DON'T JUST COUNT YOUR HOURS

MAKE YOUR HOURS COUNT

The Essential Guide to Volunteering & Community Service

Kristin E. Joos, Ph.D. • **Alana J. Rush**

Don't Just Count Your Hours, Make Your Hours Count:

The Essential Guide to Volunteering & Community Service

Kristin E. Joos, Ph.D.   Alana J. Rush

Table of Contents

About the Book

When I was 25 years old, finishing my dissertation that I defended in 2003 to earn my Ph.D., one of my most respected professors and advisors asked me, "Do you think students should be required to do community service? You make a strong case for the advantages of community service and volunteering, for the organizations and communities served as well as the students themselves, so—tell me, do you think the benefits are so strong that community service should be mandatory for all students?"

I paused, my mind running wild with thoughts and possible responses. I took a deep breath. "No. I mean, yes. I mean, no."

Then I started again. "No, I don't think schools or the government should require students to do community service. As much as I advocate the benefits of community service, service-learning, and volunteering, if you require students to do anything, they may resist, and then you lose what could have been a fantastic opportunity. I *do* hope that every student gets involved in his or her community."

I have reflected on this question and my response over the past ten years, during which time I have taught thousands of students who have performed approximately 50,000 hours of local community service as part of service-learning experiences integrated into my courses. I have read countless student papers about their experiences. They often mention having done service in high school, to meet a requirement for graduation, for the International Baccalaureate Programme, or to earn a Florida Bright Futures Scholarship. Many had not become involved in community service in college until taking my class. Most confess they were hesitant about fitting the required hours into their already busy schedules and apprehensive about finding the "right" organization with which to volunteer.

At the semester's end, with projects done and graded, I inevitably receive emails from students thanking me, telling me their service-learning experience was the most beneficial activity they engaged in all semester, and that it meant a lot to them to apply what they were learning in the classroom to the "real world" while volunteering. Many tell moving stories and share their decision to continue volunteering with the organization beyond their required hours. The students' accounts all have similar themes—volunteering makes them see they are making a difference, they come to care about the people and issues they encounter, and the beneficiaries include the people they're serving as well as themselves.

They recognize personal transformation and are excited to apply what was learned through volunteering to their future education and careers.

Earlier in the semester, prior to such appreciative and thoughtful sentiments, I am often bombarded with emails and foot traffic in my office from students asking over and over: *How do I find an organization that fits my interests? my schedule? my transportation needs? How do I get in touch with someone at the organization to sign up? What do I need to know before my first visit? How do I log my hours and get them approved? What do I do if this is boring?*

This guide was created in hopes of answering such questions. By providing students with basic information about volunteering, they can more readily graduate to more significant questions: *How does what I see while volunteering connect to the social issues we're studying in class? What is this experience teaching me about social, environmental, and economic issues, both locally and globally? What am I learning about myself, and what will I carry with me while planning my future as an active community member, leader, and change agent?*

This guide is dedicated to students who overcome fear, apprehension, or reluctance in order to open themselves to new experiences through community service, service-learning, and volunteerism. We commend you for being courageous, motivated, bright, and enthusiastic, and for giving your time, talent, and energy in hopes of creating positive social, environmental, and economic change. We do not believe young people are, as the cliché says, "the leaders of tomorrow." You can be, *and are,* leaders today.

Kristin E. Joos, Ph.D.

We would like to thank...

Our friend Jenn Fauls for introducing us.

Our much respected and admired friend and colleague, Dr. Colette Taylor, who served as the first director of the Center for Leadership & Service at UF; and Professor Stephanie Evans, for sharing her passion for and expertise in service-learning with us.

Samantha Baer, a most amazing young, dynamic, change-maker, who gave us much appreciated encouragement.

Those who helped us with the seemingly impossible task of choosing a title: Fatima AlBader, Alex Alghussain, Brittany Bruce, Aura Cely, Jessica Cole, Hiranya Derasari, Lance Guerrwitz, Eduardo Hariton, Katie Heroux, Arial Landry, Jackie Lender, Celia Lewis, Abhi Lokesh, Blake Matison, Trisha Macrae, Melissa Miller, Katya Prosvirkina, Wade Senti, Blaire Shoor, David Valancy, Jannae White, and Stefan Wolff.

Those who lent their stories and quotes to our work: Anabel Bacon, Zahra Bhaiwala, Matt Cranney, Rachel Cohen, Mary Barrett Doyle, Callahan Fore, Eli Grober, Harrison Hart, Andy Housiaux, Kelley Kostamo, Trisha Macrae, Lily Shaffer, Howard Sticklor, Jackie Wallace, Tori Wilmarth, and Patrick Wolber.

DeeDee Rasmussen & Courtney Geinert with Florida Campus Compact.

Tracey Reeves & Andrew Perrone and the Center for Leadership & Service at the University of Florida, and Angela Garcia of Gator Nonprofit Professionals.

Chad Green, Carlos Hoyt, Raj Mundra, and the Office of Community Service at Phillips Academy Andover.

Cathryn Berger Kaye for sharing her expertise and advice, which resulted in a much stronger manuscript, and for her insightful and comprehensive editing.

Rebecca Brown for asking a 15-year-old Kristin to chair a youth "service team," encouraging her to share with others her enthusiasm for getting involved in the community.

Professor Emeritus Arnie Heggestad, the founding Director of the Center for Entrepreneurship & Innovation at UF, whose support was the catalyst making our Innovative Sustainability & Social Impact Initiative a reality;

and Jamie Kraft, the Managing Director of CEI, for his continued support of developing experiential learning projects to create opportunities that incentivize community service among graduate students.

Professor & Chair of Sociology at the University of Florida, Dr. Connie Shehan, for her ongoing mentoring, advice, and tremendous support, especially with regard to our efforts to empower students through applied sociology and service-learning assignments.

Amy Haines for sharing her meticulous editing skills. She is a much appreciated and amazingly gifted wordsmith whose aesthetic sense transforms disarray into perfection.

Scott Fore and Wesley Barnett of Treetop Software for tasking us with writing this guide. Without your request, resources, and pending deadline, this guide would still be an idea in our heads rather than a reality and resource to share with students.

Kristin E. Joos, Ph.D.
Alana J. Rush
June 2011

This book is dedicated to the Memory of Dr. Sherri Aversa, the Founding Director of the North Central Florida AIDS Network. She warmly mentored Kristin as a 16-year-old volunteer, kindly explaining, you should use your gifts and talents and *make your hours count*.

Chapter 1: Why Volunteer

"Volunteering is not just an act of selflessness; it's also an act of self-empowerment and self-development. And it's just so much fun."

–Eli Grober, Columbia University

Callahan Fore is a 19-year-old sophomore at the University of Florida and a social entrepreneur. At 15, Cal attended a high school that required him to complete 50 community-service hours each year. While Cal and his classmates were eager to participate and not afraid of hard work, they had no idea where to begin. He heard that a local church was sponsoring a trip to the Appalachian Mountains to repair and renovate homes of elderly and disabled people in rural, impoverished areas (www.asphome.org). Cal had a memorable time helping a family in Kentucky, but was perplexed as to why he had to travel to complete his service hours, since he was sure there were needs in his local community.

Cal began to wonder if there was some way to create an online network to share community service opportunities.

In summer 2007, Cal attended the Young Entrepreneurs for Leadership & Sustainability Summer Program (www.ufyoungentrepreneurs.org). The help and guidance he found there turned his idea into a reality. Cal and a team of friends launched a website called www.sweatmonkey.org. It was a funny name, but Cal was raised to believe in sweat equity, and his father teased him, calling Cal and his friends "monkeys." In 2011, the team decided a name change was in order and **NobleHour** was born, a more fitting name for the platform Cal and his friends had created. Now at www.NobleHour.com, students can search and find opportunities for community service, internships, and jobs right in their local communities.

As an added feature, **NobleHour.com** tracks hours and compiles a student's involvement into a résumé that can be downloaded and submitted for college and graduate school admissions or job applications. **NobleHour's** mission is to connect students with their communities—so local organizations get much needed help and students are given opportunities to develop valuable professional and leadership skills, and experience their efficacy now.

Many scholarships are available for students who demonstrate a strong commitment to community service. For example:

Bonner Scholars
The Bonner Scholars Program seeks to transform the lives of students at 27 specific colleges and universities as well as their campuses, local communities, and nation by providing access to education and opportunities to serve. To achieve this mission, the Bonner Foundation provides four-year community service scholarships to approximately 1500 students, the Bonner Scholars, annually. Scholarships are given to individuals who demonstrate high financial need and commitment to service.
http://www.bonner.org/campus/bsp/howtoapply.htm

Prudential Spirit of the Community Awards
The Prudential Spirit of Community Awards program is the United States' largest youth recognition program based exclusively on volunteer community service. The program was created in 1995 by Prudential in partnership with the National Association of Secondary School Principals (NASSP) to honor middle level and high school students for outstanding service to others at the local, state, and national level. Students are encouraged to complete an online application by November 2.
http://spirit.prudential.com/view/page/soc/14830

Kohls Kids Who Care Scholarship Program
The Kohl's Kids Who Care® Scholarship Program recognizes and rewards young volunteers (ages 6-18) whose efforts have made a positive impact on their communities. To date, Kohls has recognized more than 11,000 kids and awarded more than $2.2 million in scholarships and prizes, ranging from $50 Kohl's Gift Cards to $1,000 or $10,000 scholarships. Winners are chosen based on the project, benefits and outcomes. The deadline is usually in March.
http://www.kohlskids.com

For more scholarship resources, check out Scholarships.com's "Community Service Scholarships" list.

Points to Remember

- Don't just count your hours, make your hours count.
- Engage in meaningful service.
- Be open to new experiences.
- If you're feeling nervous, apprehensive, reluctant, or just lazy... stop procrastinating and *just do it.*

Approximately 14.6 million K–12 students in the U.S. engaged in community service in 2007–2008[i] to fulfill requirements for high school graduation or to be eligible for merit-based scholarships. Over the past decade, and especially within the past few years, the number of college students engaging in community service and service-learning has increased dramatically[ii], as colleges and universities across the nation have implemented new offices and programs to foster students' engagement in their communities. Some colleges now require community-service involvement for graduation and are integrating this information into students' academic transcripts. In fact, federal legislation proposed by the Obama administration in 2010 has set a goal for all high school students to complete 50 hours of community service each year[iii] and for all students to complete 100 hours of service while in college[iv].

With literally millions of youth volunteers, it is surprising how few resources exist to help educate and prepare them in their efforts to contribute to their communities. Some nonprofit organizations and community agencies require volunteers to complete anywhere from a few minutes to a few hours of training, while many organizations have no required training. Imagine stepping into any position without even an orientation session!

There are a variety of service-related tasks that volunteers do, including but not limited to:

arts, crafts, music

companionship

construction & repair

direct client support

environmental cleanups

general office work (filing, copying)

mentoring

planning fundraisers

program/event planning

receptionist (answering phones & greeting visitors)

research

special projects

sports

translation

tutoring

updating membership databases

website design & maintenance

A handful of books[v] and a few websites[vi] offer students resources to prepare for volunteering. We discuss these resources in Chapter 10.

Don't Just Count Your Hours, Make Your Hours Count: The Essential Guide to Volunteering & Community Service is an up-to-date guide for high school and college students, articulating the basics of what students need to know to have positive meaningful volunteer experiences and maximize their contributions to the organizations they serve. Here, student volunteers can find basic information, advice, and tips. This book is intended to be most useful for students fulfilling scholarship or graduation requirements, as well as those engaged in service-learning as part of a class or course (see Chapter 8 for more on service-learning). This book also serves as the curriculum for the online Volunteer Training Certification. With accurate and adequate information that prepares students to be effective volunteers, we empower and inspire young people to be leaders in their communities through the experience of service.

Are you getting ready to volunteer? Have you volunteered in the past and have some idea about what to expect? Or is this totally new, and you're wondering what you've signed up for? Millions of students like you, in schools and universities across the United States, are becoming involved in community service and service-learning. Whether for a class, graduation, scholarship, or to boost your résumé, the rewards go beyond satisfying the requirement. Maybe you're eager for a new experience. Perhaps you want to learn about social, environmental, and economic issues and related careers through personal involvement. Whatever the reason, volunteering has the potential for deep reciprocal benefits as you create positive change in the world, and you change as well.

What are Benefits of Community Service?

Experience! Participating in community service provides essential real-world experience. You may better determine courses to study in college, or discover a potential career path. Volunteering helps develop and improve skills that prepare you for the world of work.

Connections! As a volunteer, you meet people in your community who can be of help in the future—writing letters of recommendation for college and scholarship applications, or acting as references for internships and job applications. They can also help in your job search. The more people you know, the bigger your network!

Perspective! While volunteering, you may meet people of varying backgrounds and learn about issues and topics you've never encountered. These new people and experiences may impact the way you view and understand the world, and engaging in community service can influence your future plans for making a contribution to the world. Many professionals find a way to offer their skills pro bono to organizations because they volunteered along the way.

Continuity! Learn from older generations. As 77 million baby boomers retire, it's a great opportunity to learn from them. Intergenerational learning can be enriching, so seek out experiences that enable this to occur.

Voice! Volunteering gives you opportunities to have your voice heard. During your service experience, you may be asked to share your ideas, opinions, and thoughts. Your feedback could directly impact the future of the organization, so speak up!

Adapted from the "Benefits of Community Based Service Learning" factsheet, courtesy of Learn & Serve America's National Service-Learning Clearinghouse, which highlights the outcomes of extensive research on the benefits of community service and service-learning for students, organizations, and the communities they serve; found in the Appendix on page 72.

Engage in Meaningful Service

We all want our time to be spent in a way that has meaning and purpose. Busywork and menial tasks can seem "boring," but envelopes must be stuffed with letters to members or potential donors, and someone must make copies, file papers, answer phones, staff information desks, reply to emails, sort through mail, and complete other seemingly "mindless" though necessary tasks. When we understand the *context* of our work—for example, invitations being mailed for a fundraiser necessary for the organization to complete their mission—the task changes from "boring" to more *meaningful*. Similarly, an activity that begins with high interest, such as tutoring, can become tedious with repetition. The obligation is ours to replenish our sense of purpose and refresh our intentions. Remember, every effort made when volunteering impacts both the people served and ourselves. The more authentic meaning we add, the more we will see how our time, talent, and dedicated work create *actual change in the world*. Chapter 7 discusses the importance of understanding the big picture, including tips for staying motivated.

Be Open to New Experiences

For even a seasoned volunteer, much of your community-service experience will be new. You will encounter new people and experiences, in new places and settings. For some, this sounds frightening, intimidating, and even overwhelming. For others, it sounds like an adventure waiting to unfold. The reality is usually a little of both. When volunteering, you may get to know people from various backgrounds, with different beliefs, habits, customs, ways of talking, and dress. When encountering diversity, some people retreat to what is familiar and comfortable, and in doing so they may miss out on opportunity. When encountering new people and experiences, choose to be open and curious, and reach out to others with warmth. Soon, what was unfamiliar and even strange will become what you most look forward to. We discuss this in more detail in Chapter 5. Hesitancy about new experiences is what keeps many people from taking the leap to reaching out and helping others. If you are feeling nervous, apprehensive, reluctant, or just lazy... stop procrastinating and, like the Nike ad says, *Just Do It*!

This guide offers advice on how to have positive, productive, rewarding, and fun volunteer experiences. We begin by dispelling myths about community service and reviewing things to keep in mind before you begin. We then discuss how to find volunteer opportunities and offer tips and suggestions for contacting organizations and preparing for your first visit. Next we offer advice on how to be a "volunteer extraordinaire," maintain your motivation and energy, and *make your hours count*. Finally we share suggestions for responsibly coming to closure with a volunteer commitment. At the end of each section, you will also find Additional Resources for more information.

Additional Resources:

Ashoka's Youth Venture: http://www.genv.net
Ashoka's Youth Venture helps teams of people start new youth-led organizations. GenV.net is a website with access to resources for coming up with ideas to start social ventures and provides resources to support them.

Global Youth Action Network: www.youthlink.org
GYAN is a large network of youth organizations in over 190 countries. The Network is known for its role in increasing youth participation within the United Nations System.

National Youth Leadership Council: www.nylc.org
NYLC has as its mission empowering youth to transform themselves from recipients of information and resources into valuable, contributing members of a democracy through service-learning. Every year, about 2000 people attend the National Service-Learning Conference, and NYLC has been a leader in establishing the current national standards for K–12 service-learning.

NobleHour.com: http://www.NobleHour.com

Noble Hour is an online community engagement platform that allows students to find opportunities, log their hours, and track and measure their impact.

Youth Service America: www.ysa.org

YSA is committed to improving communities by increasing the number and diversity of 5-25 year olds involved in their communities. YSA runs public mobilization campaigns, like Global Youth Service Day, provides funding and awards for service endeavors, and conducts training events for young people and educators around the country.

YouthNoise: www.youthnoise.org

YouthNoise is an online forum with more than 170,000 registered users from all 50 states and 176 countries around the world. YouthNoise primarily works with low-income and under-represented youth ages 13–25. YouthNoise partners with Link TV and the *Just 1 Click* campaign to support youth service efforts virtually.

"Be the change you wish to see in the world."

Mohandas Gandhi
*Leader of the Indian independence movement and
proponent of nonviolent civil resistance*

"Never doubt that a small group of thoughtful, committed citizens can change the world. Indeed, it is the only thing that ever has."

Margaret Mead
Cultural anthropologist

Chapter 2: Look Before You Leap

"Volunteering is like anything else in life. You won't necessarily start out being good at it. Ultimately, your commitment, perseverance, and passion will lead the way to meaningful work."

Harrison Hart, Dartmouth College

At a start-of-term volunteer fair, a soon-to-be volunteer was overheard saying, "I love animals. Playing with puppies and cuddling kitties isn't work to me, it's fun! I'll volunteer at the Humane Society. Great, that was easy."

The volunteer signed up and on his first day, discovered that he had been assigned to work on a fundraising campaign to support rescuing strays, rather than working directly with animals, which is what he assumed he would be doing... Someone didn't do their homework!

PRACTICAL TIPS:

✓ Know the difference among volunteer opportunities: direct vs. indirect, team vs. individual, structured vs. unstructured

✓ Ask questions about **supervision, structure of the volunteer program,** and **type of volunteer work**

✓ If someone recommends a site, ask him or her WHY they recommend it—great people? valuable learning experience? hands-on? Also ask WHY it had personal importance.

Points to Remember

• Ask questions before you start volunteering and figure out what you're looking for.

• There are many different types of volunteering—it's really important to find the *right fit* or to accept the situation and be flexible.

• Do your homework!

Myths of Volunteering

If you're not being paid, you can come and go as you please. Your volunteer placement site and the people you are serving depend on you to be punctual and reliable. By showing up late, you limit your ability to contribute and you could become a hindrance to the agency. Behave as an employee at a job and garner the respect you earn. Consider your commitment carefully and sign up to volunteer *only* if you can follow through.

You should only volunteer for an organization you're already passionate about. Consider this an opportunity to learn about something completely different that you're interested in pursuing down the line, or that piques your curiosity. Volunteering is a great low-risk way to explore and discover new interests.

"I don't like kids, old people, or animals, so there's no way I'll like volunteering." Not all volunteering is the same. From work with pro bono legal service organizations, to building houses for Habitat for Humanity, to serving as a docent at an art museum, volunteer opportunities are as diverse as your imagination. Whether you like music, art, politics, sports, chess, or _____ (fill in the blank), there is an opportunity to match your interests.

All opportunities are created equally. Some nonprofit organizations are better prepared to handle volunteers than others. Contact other volunteers from the agency to ask about their experiences. Do your best to assess whether the organization has the capacity to handle volunteers—this affords you the best opportunity to learn, participate, and contribute to an important cause. Questions about the orientation program or how long usually volunteers stay with the organization can get you started.

How to Find the Right Fit

Volunteering is based on relationships, specifically the relationship between you and the organization. To figure out what's best for you, it's important to know about **the volunteer site** and about **what you're looking for.**

Isn't that a bit *SELFISH?*

It may seem counterintuitive to be looking out for yourself during this process. You may be asking yourself, "Aren't I here to volunteer? Shouldn't it be about the organization and not ME?" Check this out: There are over 1.8 Million[vii] registered nonprofits in the United States alone, so:

     a) you have options, and
     b) there's no way you could help all of them.

You have to choose. With this choice, you're trying to maximize impact, so look for something you'll enjoy doing and identify an environment in which you'll thrive. You and the people you work alongside and serve will ALL benefit! **In this case, being a bit selfish ultimately allows you to be more altruistic.**

Something else to remember: Organizations are made of *people*. Observing the working environment and interfacing with some of the staff will help put a literal "face" on what the place is all about and whether you are a good fit.

Volunteering as Part of a Program or On Your Own

Many schools, universities, and nonprofits run volunteer programs. When you sign up, you are often volunteering in a small group run by a volunteer leader. This type of program provides great one-on-one support, the opportunity to socialize with other volunteers, and often includes training or orientation---a great way to start volunteering. Examples: A group of musicians performing at elderly homes, a group of students visiting an animal shelter every other week, or volunteers who sign up to help with a kids' sports program every Saturday morning for eight weeks.

Another option is to sign up on your own to volunteer with an organization. You might volunteer in a second-grade classroom or help out at a legal aid office once a week. If on your own, you'll have to rely on initiative to ensure you're jumping into your work, getting to know the people around you, and taking advantage of every situation. As an independent volunteer, you have the potential for more responsibility and individualized opportunities, and will need to be proactive in seeking out tasks and following up on projects. Any initiative you take will pay off!

Questions to ask:

How many volunteers work with your organization? How much interaction will I have with other volunteers? How long have you had a volunteer program? What kind of orientation program do you have? How long do volunteers typically stay with your organization?

Direct vs. Indirect Service

The range of volunteer opportunities available includes everything from volunteering in an office for a nonprofit organization to playing with small children or caring for animals, and everything in between. The service you do can be characterized as **direct** or **indirect**:

Direct Service:
Volunteers work directly with the population (this can include the environment or animals) the organization is serving. Examples: Serving dinner at a meal kitchen, reading to a child in a classroom, coaching kids with the Special Olympics, gathering water samples for testing.

Indirect Service:
Volunteers assist without seeing the recipients of what they provide. Examples: Stocking a food pantry, developing a database for an agency to keep track of donors, redoing a nonprofit's website.

Both direct and indirect service are necessary to meet community needs. Many organizations provide hybrid opportunities, like volunteering for an environmental organization's office two days a week and going into their community garden with kids once a week. In addition to direct and indirect service, some volunteers participate in **Research** or **Advocacy** work in order to further social change. Research focuses on solving a community problem or effecting social change by studying issues or situations and providing data to decision-makers, evaluating new and existing programs, or creating qualitative and quantitative research tools. Advocacy addresses the needs of a community by promoting policy-level change or educating the public about a specific problem. Volunteers doing advocacy work might work with local political organizations, lobby elected politicians about the rights of people who are underrepresented, or write articles for an awareness-raising magazine.

Questions to ask:

Who do you serve? Will I be working directly with any populations? What is the impact of your organization? Are their in-office needs where my skills would be helpful?

Supervision & Training

Developing a relationship with your supervisor is vitally important. This person will be your guide within the organization. Whether something goes well or badly, this person will ultimately help you navigate your volunteer experience. Find out how much contact you'll have with your supervisor and how to get in touch with him or her when needed.

Questions to ask:

Who will be supervising me? Will that person be onsite? How much training must volunteers complete before beginning? When/where does that training take place? Do we have ongoing meetings for review?

Vision, Mission, History

What this organization does is an important part of your experience. Knowing the history and background, the size, the way the place is organized, and the overall purpose is critical for meaningful participation. Be sure to do your homework; often much of this information is on their website, or in brochures or annual reports. Being informed before you arrive let's them know you cared enough to be prepared. Find out about who is served and also about the people who work *for* the organization. This gathered knowledge will give you a sense of what volunteering there may be like.

Questions to ask:

When was the organization founded? What is your mission? How long have you had volunteers? How would you describe your impact?

Investigating

You've just received a list of questions and considerations for a volunteer site. As noted, much information may be available on the organization's website, in their documents, or from prior volunteers. Other answers are only available through being on site and interacting. Plus, what a website says is the organizational mission may differ from what is stated when you ask someone during a visit.

Knowing about the site is part of building excitement and anticipation about volunteering and replacing myths with what is more likely to happen. This leads you to making a more assured commitment to volunteer. Once you finish your service, think about questions you wish you had asked at the beginning so you can learn what else to ask next time to be better informed and prepared.

Additional Resources:

http://www.campuscompact.org/

Campus Compact helps colleges engage college students as active citizens who address challenging societal issues. Over the past 20 years, Campus Compact has engaged more than 20 million students in service and service-learning. Campus Compact has a presence in states and on college campuses throughout the United States.

http://www.serve.gov/

Serve.gov is managed by the Corporation for National and Community Service as an online resource for creating and finding volunteer opportunities. *United We Serve* focuses specifically on emerging social needs resulting from the economic downturn.

"The way you get meaning into your life is to devote yourself to loving others, devote yourself to your community around you, and devote yourself to creating something that gives you purpose and meaning."

Mitch Albom
Author, journalist, and broadcaster

"To make a difference is not a matter of accident, a matter of casual occurrence of the tides. People choose to make a difference."

Maya Angelou
Author, poet, and civil rights activist

"I strive to engage and approach service with an understanding of the community I am working with and what will be most useful and meaningful for community partners as well as volunteers."

Victoria Wilmarth, Robertson Scholar at Duke University

Imagine "Sarah Student" needs to complete 75 hours of service to be awarded a scholarship for college. She has asked her parents and teachers if they have any ideas, and her mom suggested she pick up trash in a local park with Keep America Beautiful, while her teacher said she could read to children at the Pre-K program next to her high school. Although likely to fill important needs, these opportunities were not really interesting to Sarah Student. She really wanted to help plant a community garden to provide sustainable, healthy food options for low-income neighborhoods.

Sarah logged on to NobleHour.com, entered her zip code, and searched for environmental organizations. She quickly discovered that the Florida Organic Growers GIFT Gardens Program needed volunteers to help build community gardens. *Score!*

How can you be sure the organization you're working with is legitimate?

Guidestar has ratings of many nonprofits and non-governmental organizations in the United States.

http://www2.guidestar.org/rxg/give-to-charity/index.aspx

Points to Remember

- Websites can be an efficient way to find volunteer opportunities. NobleHour.com is a great place to start!
- Community-service centers on campuses and counselor offices in high school frequently have volunteer postings and may have vetted the agency.
- Trusted adults like parents, teachers, coaches, and neighbors may also have good suggestions.
- Volunteering can be more fun when done with friends.

You want to be a volunteer. You need community-service hours—for school, a scholarship, or just to make a positive contribution. You know of an elderly neighbor whose lawn you could mow or a new mother who could use your help running errands, but you also know that in order to get "credit" for the hours you volunteer, your work must be completed with a nonprofit organization. Many students have no idea where to search for volunteer opportunities. The purpose of this chapter is to provide resources for searching and successfully finding community-service opportunities.

Volunteering Online:

This is ideal when you really can't leave your house, but want to help others.

http://www.onlinevolunteering.org
http://www.utexas.edu/lbj/rgk/serviceleader/

The Internet

The Internet makes finding volunteer opportunities easier than ever. Many websites are designed to assist students connect with organizations that need volunteers. NobleHour.com is one such site. Students enter their zip code and the site generates a list of local organizations prepared for volunteers. Opportunities can be sorted by distance, mission of the organization, or task. NobleHour.com even provides an *E-hours* feature, which students use to log their hours and generate a service-learning résumé or transcript that documents their community-service endeavors.

Other websites include:

- 1800 Volunteer: http://www.1-800-volunteer.org/
- All for Good: http://www.allforgood.org/
- America's Natural and Cultural Resources Volunteer Portal: http://www.volunteer.gov/gov/
- Idealist Volunteer Opportunities: http://idealist.org/if/as/vol
- U Give: http://www.ugive.org
- Volunteer Match: http://www.volunteermatch.org

Familiar Organizations

Think of organizations you already know—like the Red Cross or Habitat for Humanity. Does volunteering with an organization that is a household name interest you? If so, great! If you're not sure, ask people who have volunteered with those organizations in the past to share their stories.

Ask people you know if they know of any organizations in need of help—friends, parents, teachers, coaches, neighbors, and other trusted adults. They may remind you of familiar places you just didn't consider, yet.

Your friends may have already met a service-hours requirement or have taken a course that requires service. Where did they volunteer and what was it like? Organizations often ask current or prior volunteers to spread the word about the needs of the organization and help find future volunteers. A reference from a friend who enjoyed volunteering with an organization is usually a good indicator that you might have a positive experience, too.

Service Centers

Many communities have Volunteer Centers or organizations that collectively post volunteer opportunities for local organizations; check a local phone book or online. Does your school have a central place where volunteer opportunities are posted—in a counselor's office or community-service center on campus?

Trusted Advisors

Asking trusted advisors may be a bit time-consuming and even intimidating, but doing so can reap maximum rewards. Someone you admire—a teacher or professor, relative, Big Brother, college advisor, or neighbor—can tell you about the needs of the organizations with which they work. You may find an environmental organization that needs people to pull trash from local creeks, an animal shelter that needs people to cuddle kittens and puppies until they find permanent homes, a homeless shelter that needs people to serve dinner, or a tutoring program that needs people to help children with homework. The more people you ask, the more likely you are to discover rewarding opportunities. Then share what you find out with friends—volunteering can be fun with a partner.

However you discover a recommendation of an organization, be sure to ask *why* people are making this recommendation to gain a better idea as to why this place might be a great fit for *you*.

Additional Resources:

http://www.liveunited.org

Live United is a campaign run by United Way. LiveUnited focuses on education, income stability, and healthy lives through campaigns, awards, corporate partnerships, and other efforts.

http://www.NobleHour.com

Noble Hour is an online community engagement platform that allows students to find opportunities, log their hours, and track and measure their impact.

"Don't ask yourself what the world needs; ask yourself what makes you come alive. And then go and do that. Because what the world needs is people who have come alive."

Howard Thurman
Theologian, author, and civil rights leader

"Those who are not looking for happiness are the most likely to find it, because those who are searching forget that the surest way to be happy is to seek happiness for others."

Martin Luther King, Jr.
Baptist minister and civil rights leader

*"My ARC Buddy Jimmy says,
'ARC is like jello, not too hard, but always fun.'"*

Matt Cranney, Tulane University
ARC is a program for high school students and buddies with special needs

David, a high school student, coordinates a volunteer program at his school that works with a local youth development organization. He brings elementary children to the high school for after-school tutoring.

The nonprofit youth development organization is well known and respected in the community. The director, however, prefers phone or in-person communication over emails. David was used to communicating with his peers and teachers via email. He first attempted to contact the director via email and got no response. He waited a few days and emailed again. He then complained that it was impossible to reach the director and began to give up on the project.

However, after speaking to the service-learning coordinator at his school, he learned that making a phone call was the best way to reach the director and that he would usually get a response within a few minutes of calling. Later that same day, David called the director of the youth development organization, they spoke, and within the hour they had a game plan for tutoring to begin the following day.

David learned that it is essential to know what communication method is appropriate when working in a more professional relationship. For some, email will be preferred; for others, a good ol' fashioned reliable phone call.

Points to Remember

- Be patient, persistent, and polite.
- Email may not be the best method of communication. Try calling during office hours.
- Remember that volunteer coordinators might be volunteers themselves, so instead of waiting for a response, call again.

You have successfully found an organization needing volunteer help, which is a great beginning. To complete your hours, there is much more to be done. Students new to community service are often unsure how to go about contacting the organization to begin volunteering. In this chapter, we provide tips and advice for contacting organizations and initiating your relationship.

YouthNoise.com

YouthNoise empowers young leaders to act for causes locally, nationally, and globally. By offering online and offline tools, YouthNoise equips youth to turn ideas into action on a wide range of social issues—from health to education, from violence to poverty. With158,000 registered users from all 50 states and 176 countries, YouthNoise has established a virtual meeting place for the next generation of activists.

Whether you found the opportunity online or by word of mouth, contact the organization to learn more about their needs and determine if it's a good fit for your interests, talents, and abilities.

If you found the opportunity online, it was probably accompanied by contact information—an email address, phone number, and perhaps the name of a contact person or volunteer coordinator or manager. Use the contact information provided to get in touch with the organization.

If you found the opportunity by word of mouth, ask whoever referred you whether they have the name of a contact person. Otherwise do an online search or use the phone book to find the phone number and ask for the volunteer coordinator as a place to begin.

As stated previously, always do background research on the organization, and prepare a list of questions; remember to review the questions provided in Chapter 2.

One common mistake students make when initially contacting an organization is to send an email and wait days or weeks for a response. Many agencies only check email once a week, especially organizations staffed primarily by volunteers. Checking email so rarely may seem incomprehensible to those of us who check email on our smartphones multiple times throughout the day, but it's the reality for many underfunded nonprofit organizations.

No response to an email? After waiting a few days, pick up the phone and call during standard office hours: 8am–5pm. Avoid calling first thing in the morning, between 12 and 1pm, or just before closing, since organizations may be busier at those times. Remember, agencies are often understaffed and the people there are overworked. You may need to call two to three times a day to reach the right person. Don't wait for them to get back to you—actively pursue getting in touch with them.

Be persistent, patient, and polite. Persistency and patience may seem contradictory—but they are not. Be persistent by not waiting more than one day before calling back, and be patient, polite, kind, and understanding in your demeanor. When you get in touch with someone at the organization, no matter how long it has taken you or how frustrated you might be, be polite, gracious and respectful of their time. Always ask, "Is this a good time to talk, or can we make an appointment?" to show a sensitivity to this person's time and schedule.

Introduce yourself as a student interested in volunteering with their organization. Ask about volunteer opportunities and describe any requirements you have for this placement from your school, instructor, or supervisor. Based on the amount of time available for this conversation, ask your top questions and arrange a time for a visit. We discuss this in more detail in Chapter 5.

Additional Resources:

http://www.NobleHour.com

Noble Hour is an online community engagement platform that allows students to find opportunities, log their hours, and track and measure their impact.

http://unitedweserve.causecast.org/

Causecast is an online global community and social action network that empowers individuals, businesses, and nonprofits with media and tools that transform interest into action.

"Never, never, never, never give up."

Winston Churchill
Former British Prime Minister

"How wonderful it is that no one need wait a single moment before starting to change the world."

Anne Frank
Diarist, victim of the Holocaust

Chapter 5: Preparing for Your First Visit

"The key to affecting change is to never lose the shock and fury that hit you when you are first exposed to injustice. Combine that with passion, curiosity, and excitement and you will be unstoppable."

Anabel Bacon, Columbia University

The C.H.A.M.P.S. mentoring program invites college students to mentor elementary students in Gainesville, Florida. Kelley Kostamo, the program's director, always forewarns volunteers with the story of one college mentor, who arrived for her first day wearing a tank-top and low-rise jeans—perfectly appropriate attire for her classes at college.

She and her new second grade mentee sat down to get to know each other and, unbeknownst to her, the combination of her low-cut jeans and the elementary-sized tables and chairs meant that the back of her red underwear was visible to a lunchroom full of elementary school students who had no qualms about pointing, laughing, and becoming quite distracted. Needless to say, the volunteer was very conscious of her attire for the rest of the term.

Points to Remember

- Schedule your first visit and confirm how long you will be there.
- Ask what to expect.
- Ask what to wear or bring.
- Get directions.
- Bring an open mind.
- Instead of interacting only with people "like you," challenge yourself outside of your comfort zone and extend yourself to meet new people from diverse backgrounds and life experiences.

Not In Our Town (NIOT) is a national movement that encourages and connects people who are responding to hate and working to build more inclusive communities. NOIT uses the power of media, grassroots events, educational outreach, and online activities to help communities talk to and learn from each other. Together, NOIT communities share stories and strategies about how to foster safety, inclusion, and acceptance.
http://www.niot.org

Wear & Pack
for various service experiences:

Creek Cleanups

- ☐ clothes you can get dirty, muddy, and possibly stained
- ☐ close-toed shoes
- ☐ gloves
- ☐ sunscreen & mosquito repellant
- ☐ a big yard-size trash bag
- ☐ an extra change of clothes

Playground Renovation

- ☐ clothes you can move easily in and get dirty and possibly paint-stained
- ☐ close-toed shoes
- ☐ sunscreen & hat/cap
- ☐ gloves
- ☐ water to drink

Visit to a Retirement Center or Nursing Home

- ☐ business casual attire, no short-shorts, nice shirt without logo
- ☐ an extra sweater, they are sometimes cold
- ☐ perhaps something to share like baked goods, arts and crafts, or a game

Tutoring or Reading to Children at a School

- ☐ appropriate clothing, casual, but no short shorts or tank-tops
- ☐ think of a few questions you could ask kids as conversation starters, like what is your favorite movie? subject in school? color? food?
- ☐ One of your favorite children's stories
- ☐ perhaps a small game, like cards, Uno, Go Fish
- ☐ a smile

After successfully finding a service opportunity and contacting the organization to confirm that it's a good fit for you, there are a few more considerations before you volunteer for the first time. Most students are eager to get started and jump right in, but wait! In this chapter, we outline tips and suggestions for how to best prepare for your first volunteer experience with an organization. Even seasoned volunteers benefit from a reminder to approach each new community-service experience prepared and with an open mind.

You would always show up at a job interview with a well-prepared résumé and wearing appropriate attire. You attend a party knowing who it's for, what to wear, and if you're expected to bring something. You study or at least review questions before taking the SAT. It is the same with showing up as a volunteer—before you actually do the service, you need to know what is expected of you.

A few common-sense tips will help you be prepared (and possibly avoid that awkward "if only I had . . ." thought from creeping up afterwards):

Schedule your first visit: You may have already done this when you contacted the organization (see Chapter 4); if not, contact them again and confirm they are expecting you on the scheduled day and time. Be sure you find out how long they would like you to stay. If this is different from what you need for your class or requirements, have that discussion now.

Ask what to expect: What types of activities will you be engaging in— sitting in an office? doing manual labor outside? playing with children indoors and/or out? These questions are important, as they help you to know how to prepare yourself.

Ask what to wear and/or bring: Even if you think what you wear doesn't matter, you may be surprised to find the organization has a dress code or that some clothing items are unacceptable. Clearly, if you will be working outside, you need to dress appropriately. In winter, you will need to dress warmly. In the summer, they may suggest you dress for comfort, but instead of wearing flip-flops, you may need to wear sneakers for safety, especially if you are working with mowers or tools of any kind, so always double-check about footwear. Many organizations, like hospitals, are often quite specific about what volunteers should wear. Your favorite short shorts and tank-top may be your "normal" attire however if you suddenly find out you will be painting, chances are your "favorites" will get stained. Since standard dress codes vary depending on the specific volunteering endeavors, always (always, always) ask before you show up!

And what to bring? Volunteers typically supply their own water (a refillable container is best) and lunch, especially if you will be working for more than a few hours. Depending on the nature of your volunteer work, you may need to bring specific items, like a notebook and pen, arts & crafts supplies, tools, or trash bags and gloves. You may also need a photo ID, your social security number, or some other official form, like proof of immunization, especially if you are volunteering in a health care setting. Ask in advance so you are prepared when you arrive.

If you are unable to get an answer to your question about dress code, and you know you will *not* be working outside, wear "business casual" and bring a water bottle.

Get directions: Check the organization's website for a map to their location, or call for clear driving directions. Write them down. Tip: Drive by a few days in advance to double check location and driving time. Taking the bus? Same idea. Plan ahead.

Be prepared to complete application forms or paperwork: You may be asked to bring your driver's license, student/school identification card, state identification card, or other form of photo ID. You may also be asked to bring your Social Security card and give your fingerprints, as some organizations/agencies require volunteers to have a background check performed, especially when working with children. As a volunteer, you may be asked to pay for the cost of the background check (usually $15-30) and you may also have to wait a few days or weeks until the results have come in before you are permitted to begin volunteering. It is important to ask how the volunteer application process works so you are prepared to complete the required paperwork and are aware of any potential delays. *Note: If you are a minor, your parent or guardian may be asked to sign their permission for you to volunteer.* If you are on a tight schedule to meet class or school requirements, contacting an organization as soon as possible, finding out their volunteer application requirements, and getting the important forms signed, can prevent any delays or negative repercussions on your grade.

Bring an open mind: Once you know what to expect, what to wear and bring, and where you need to go, add this to your list: an open mind. One concern people often have when facing new experiences is the possibility of feeling awkward or uncomfortable in an unfamiliar environment where people, situations, activities, customs, or languages are different. Starting a new volunteer experience can be similar to attending a new school, moving to a new neighborhood, or playing a new sport, and it may be different from anything you have ever done, but with time it becomes more familiar. In just a few weeks, you may be the "expert," helping other "newbies" feel welcome and learn the ropes. You may come to realize that volunteering with the organization or agency has become an integral part of your identity, and when the time comes for you to leave, you will miss the people and tasks that have become familiar (we discuss this in Chapter 9).

It's pretty straightforward to plan for new situations by gathering information and wearing appropriate clothing. How do you prepare for new experiences that may bring unknown encounters with people who are not yet your friends or even your acquaintances? Practicing open-mindedness and cultivating an attitude of curiosity are key. If you are volunteering abroad, it is especially important to be open to new experiences, keeping in mind cultural differences may be difficult to understand or may feel quite foreign, but with time they may become familiar or even comfortable. Try to learn the local language, as doing so will help you communicate better. One of the best ways to get to know a new culture is to immerse yourself in it—while volunteering abroad you may deepen your experience by shopping at the local markets, tasting local foods, and participating in local holidays and traditions. Experienced international volunteers recommend bringing something interesting from home to share. Whether it's small gifts like t-shirts or photos of your family and friends, sharing helps bridge across cultures.

You know many people—family, friends, classmates, teachers, teammates, neighbors, community leaders—and each person is different from you in some way—appearance, age, gender, race, ethnicity, socioeconomic class, sexual orientation, language, cultural traditions, religious faiths, health, habits, abilities. When volunteering, you add to your circle of friends and acquaintances, and you may be working closely with people who appear very different from you. The more you get to know them, the more you find you have in common. We all laugh and cry, feel strong at times and weak at others, get hungry and tired, and take pleasure in something as simple as clouds in the sky or bringing a smile to someone's face. We are all humans living together on planet Earth.

One of the greatest advantages of getting involved in your community is the opportunity to encounter new experiences—people, ideas, practices, settings—that are different from what you are used to. Yes, it can be uncomfortable, uncomfortable and fun and enlightening. Keep in mind this notable quote from the movie *The Motorcycle Diaries*, "Let the world change you, and you can change the world."

Additional Resources:

Teaching Tolerance: http://www.tolerance.org/
Teaching Tolerance is an initiative of the Southern Poverty Law Center that aims to find thought-provoking news, conversation and support for those who care about diversity, equal opportunity, and respect for differences in schools.

Top Five Tips for Terrific Volunteers: http://www.NobleHour.com/5tips

"This country will not be a good place for any of us to live in unless we make it a good place for all of us to live in."

Theodore Roosevelt
26th President of the United States

"The biggest disease today is not leprosy or tuberculosis…it is the lack of love and charity; the terrible indifference towards one's neighbor."

Mother Theresa
Catholic nun, founder of the Missionaries of Charity in Calcutta

Chapter 6: How to Be a Volunteer Extraordinaire

"Standing in front of a dozen ten-year-olds on my first day, I was frightened. So, I did what I'm best at: I started making jokes. That was all it took to break the ice and set the tone for the term."

Patrick Wolber, Phillips Academy Andover

Every week, Jackie comes to the gym at her high school gym to meet up with Allison, Alyssa, Nikos, and the rest of the kids who participate in ARC, Jr.—a "best buddies" program for kids with special needs.

Jackie comes ready to play: she wears athletic clothes, leaves stress and school work behind, organizes games, and spends an hour and a half running around and having fun with the kids. Jackie didn't expect to also develop relationships with the parents and through these conversations has learned more about the kids. When ARC is over, Jackie stays at the gym to help the program leaders clean up and often engages in conversation about how the event went and how the kids are doing. If problems arise, Jackie simply relays them to the program leaders after each session.

In four years as a high school volunteer, Jackie rarely missed ARC, and always tells the kids in advance if she won't be there plus arranges for a substitute. Jackie's only concern is that she's graduating so her time with ARC will soon come to an end!

Guidelines for Inexperienced Volunteers[viii]

1. **When in Doubt, Ask for Help.** Your site supervisor understands the issues at your site and you are encouraged to approach him/her with problems or questions as they arise. Through conversation you can determine the best way to respond in challenging or uncomfortable situations.

2. **Be Punctual and Responsible.** As a volunteer, you are participating in the organization as a reliable, trustworthy, and contributing member of the team. Both your supervisor and the clients you serve rely on your punctuality and commitment to completing your service hours over the entire course of the semester.

3. **Call if You Anticipate Lateness or Absence.** Call your supervisor if you are unable to come in or if you anticipate being late. Again,

people depend on your contributed services and will be at a loss if you fail to come in as scheduled. Be mindful of their needs.

4. **Respect the Privacy of All Clients.** If you are privy to confidential information with regard to the persons with whom you are working (i.e., organizational files, diagnostics, or personal stories), it is vital that you treat it as privileged information. Discuss confidentiality with your supervisor.

5. **Be Appropriate.** You are in a work situation and are expected to treat your supervisor, co-workers, and clients with courtesy and kindness. Dress comfortably, neatly, and appropriately.

6. **Be Flexible.** The level or the intensity of the activity at a service site is not always predictable. Your flexibility to changing situations can assist the operation in running smoothly and produce positive outcomes for everyone involved.

On the other hand...

NEVER report to your service site under the influence of drugs or alcohol.

NEVER give or loan a client money or personal belongings.

NEVER give a client your address or telephone number.

NEVER make promises or commitments to a client you cannot keep.

NEVER give a client or agency representative a ride in a personal vehicle.

NEVER tolerate verbal exchange of a sexual nature or engage in behavior that might be perceived as sexual with a client or agency representative.

Use common sense and conduct yourself in a professional manner at all times. Every site has its own rules, policies, procedures, protocols, and expectations. Familiarize yourself with the inner workings of the organization.

Be sensitive to cultural contexts and open-minded to diversity, whether volunteering in your local community or abroad (as discussed in Chapter 5). More and more students are spending their spring breaks, summer vacations, or entire semesters doing service abroad, an exceptional opportunity to reinforce the importance of respecting other cultures.

Adam Finck's Ten Commandments for Volunteers[ix]

1. **Be purposeful.** Know what skills you have to contribute before you arrive on the scene.

2. **Be flexible.** This includes being prepared to do administrative grunt work.

3. **Be reflective.** Constantly question your motives. Ask yourself why you are helping, think of your motivation, and keep that at the forefront of your mind.

4. **Be receptive.** Learn as much as you can. That said, be wary of engaging for too long with volunteers who have become hardened and cynical from their work. Instead, find experienced volunteers with hope still gleaming in their eyes. Then, latch on with open ears.

5. **Be positive.** Take pride in your idealism—it's the only thing that can ward off the inevitability of cynicism's approach in your difficult environment.

6. **Be realistic.** Your idealism can be balanced only by the knowledge that you are not here to save the world, but to play one specific role and that you may never witness the effects of your efforts.

7. **Be independent.** Much of your work will depend on your personal initiative. Be a team player, but do not rely on others to guide you every step of the way.

8. **Be empathetic.** Your ability to succeed will depend entirely on your connection to and understanding of the people you work with.

9. **Be humble.** Listen. Avoid jumping to conclusions about a problem, community, or philosophy that you were recently introduced to. Act. Think. Feel. But don't come to too many conclusions—they will only halt your experiential learning process.

Quick Volunteer Tips[x]

- Be realistic about how much time and energy you will be able to devote to an organization. Start with a small commitment and build from there.

- Volunteer with others. Working for a good cause with family members, classmates, and friends can make your experience even more fun and rewarding.

- Consider your personal goals when choosing an opportunity. Volunteer work is a great way to build new skills you can use in the future. Choose an activity you know will challenge you.

- Reflect on your talents and match them with the right opportunity. For example, if you are a whiz on the Internet, think about doing Web design or research for an organization.

- Have a passion for your cause. If you really like teaching others, you might help at a school or literacy center. If animals are your thing, a local animal shelter might be a better fit. The bottom line: When you love doing something it's much easier to stay committed to it.

Points to Remember

- Volunteers are essential to the functioning of community organizations and agencies.
- Good volunteers are enthusiastic, committed, and responsible.
- Be aware, careful, and safe.
- Welcome the challenge! Have fun and feel good knowing that your efforts are helping to change the world!

Volunteer help is valuable and usually essential to nonprofit organizations and community agencies. Many organizations rely on volunteers to do what they do. An annual study by The Independent Sector valued community service at $21.36 per hour in 2010[xi]. Yep! Each hour that you volunteer, has, on average, a value of more than $20/hour for the organization you are helping. Your time, talent, and effort make an important contribution to the organization and bring great benefit the local community.

As a volunteer, you represent more than just yourself. You often represent your school, club, and even your family. Be mindful that while you might like to express your "individuality," it is important to dress and speak appropriately. In some situations, you may be asked to remove piercings or cover body art at times. Please be respectful of these requests or perhaps choose a different service assignment.

Never arrive to participate in community service while impaired. Impairment includes psychosocial or health-related distress or substance use that interferes with someone's ability to perform service activities. Psychosocial distress could be anything from major stress due to upcoming exams or deadlines, to being upset about an argument, relationship, or loss. Many substances, legal and illegal, could impair your ability to perform service. Examples include: alcohol, medications, or drugs (over-the-counter, prescription, or illegal). A cold, flu, or medical condition can interfere with your ability to be a competent volunteer or compromise the health of others. If you are unable to be fully present due to impairment or illness, inform the organization and return when you have recovered. Attempting to serve impaired or ill can be damaging; take care of yourself—to help others, you must first help yourself.

As a Volunteer, you have a Number of Rights & Responsibilities[xii]

It is your right:

- To find opportunities for meaningful volunteer work and assigned roles and tasks that best match your interests, abilities, talents, and skills
- To receive accurate information about the organization and how volunteers contribute to its mission
- To be given clear instructions and training about your role as a volunteer
- To be given choices about what you do and to feel comfortable about saying "no"
- To have your voice heard—if you have input or ideas to share as to how things might improved, your opinions will be listened to and considered
- To be treated with respect and valued for making a contribution to the organization
- To receive constructive feedback about your work and given advice as to how you can improve, if needed
- To be given the opportunity to provide the organization with feedback about your experience
- To feel safe at all times and to work in conditions where your safety, health, and well-being are not compromised
- To trust that your personal information will be kept confidential and to be trusted with confidential information if it is necessary to do your job
- To receive recognition and appreciation for the hard work you have done and your positive impact on the community

It is your responsibility:

- To participate with enthusiasm
- To be honest about what you bring to the table—your background, interests, skills, talents, motivations, availability, and any limitations

- To be reliable and punctual, and if you find yourself in a situation where you are running late or need to cancel, to let the organization know as soon as possible
- To be respectful, kind, and helpful to authority figures and other volunteers and to accept the guidance and decisions of the volunteer coordinator or staff person who supervises your work
- To perform the tasks assigned to you to the best of your ability and to ask for help as needed
- To give constructive feedback about your experience and to accept constructive feedback as to how you might improve
- To be trustworthy, honest, and maintain the confidentiality of any personal information you may be given
- To follow the organization's rules, policies, and procedures
- To be mindful and conservative when using resources provided by the organization, and avoid using these resources for personal use
- To immediately notify a staff member if you think your safety, health, or well-being is at risk
- To notify your supervisor when your commitment to the organization is coming to an end, so they can find someone to replace you, if needed

Safety

Safety is a serious matter. Volunteers should not feel their safety, health, or well-being is threatened. To assure personal safety, and that of others, avoid unnecessary risks.

Accidents & Injuries

Volunteers rarely become injured while volunteering, but unexpected accidents happen from time to time in all settings. Do your part to minimize the likelihood that you or someone else will be injured. Be alert and careful at all times. If asked to work with tools or equipment, from paper cutters to power tools, be certain you receive thorough instructions and training and, if needed, wear safety equipment.

Be aware of your environment. Keep an eye out for loose or unsteady floors, unstable handrails, slippery walkways, or other potential hazards. If you do become hurt or injured, follow the procedures you were given by your organization or agency. In case of a serious injury, call 911 immediately.

Theft

Leave items of value at home; remember a locked car is not a safe place. This includes MP3 players, expensive purses or backpacks, and jewelry. In many volunteer locations, there is little space to store personal belongings and you may work away from where your items are stored. You are no more likely to have items stolen while volunteering than while engaging in any other public activity. Your precautions minimize the likelihood of an unfortunate incident.

Sexual Harassment

Sexual harassment is defined as *any range of subtle or unsubtle persistent unwanted sexual language or behavior.* Sexual harassment is illegal. Remember that behaviors intended or perceived to be innocent or joking by one person can represent something very different to another person. Remember that the victim of sexual harassment does not have to be the person directly harassed. Anyone offended or otherwise affected by the behavior can be considered a victim of sexual harassment.

If you believe you may be being sexually harassed or if you feel uncomfortable for any reason, you can tell the harasser to stop. Doing so may be awkward or difficult, but you send the message that the behavior is unwelcome. Speak with a supervisor at your organization or agency as soon as possible so he or she can take the proper steps to address the situation and prevent this from happening again. Before a problem arises, find out who you would talk to if something came up.

When working with children, or other potentially vulnerable populations, you have a responsibility to report any news of harassment or harm being inflicted on or by the child. Laws vary from state to state, so check with your organization to learn about these laws and your organization's protocols.

For example, an elementary school child might tell a volunteer mentor about a bad situation at home. As a volunteer, you do not have to decide if statements are true, or if they are serious. If you hear about someone doing harm to themselves or others, or being harmed, always report the situation to your supervisor. Your supervisor can then take responsibility for intervention and providing help.

Cybersafety[xiii]

While most of your volunteer service will be done in person, from time to time you may use the Internet as a part of your assignments. Given that you likely spend hours each day online whether on a computer or cell phone, a few reminders about cybersafety may be helpful.

1. It is essential that you not share personal information with people you "meet" online. Most of your Facebook and MySpace "friends" are probably people you know from school or through common activities, but from time to time you may "meet" new "friends" online. Do not share your real name, address, phone number, financial information, school name, passwords, or other private information with others. Never agree to meet someone in person who you only know from the Internet.

2. Remember that your Facebook or MySpace page or any other profile you might have represents who you are to the entire world. Post only what you would feel comfortable with anyone in the whole world seeing, not just your friends. When in doubt, ask yourself whether you would want your parents or college admissions personnel or future employer to see what you are posting.

3. In addition to being safe, it's also important to be ethical—avoid hurting or bullying others while online. Only post in chat rooms, Facebook, texting, or by email what you would say to someone's face. Never use the Internet to spread gossip, bully, or hurt someone's reputation. Remember that you are in charge of your experience online. If someone makes you feel uncomfortable, you can choose to not respond to their message or post, to delete their message or post, and you are encouraged to share your concerns with a parent, supervisor, instructor, or trusted advisor.

4. Another aspect of ethics involves being honest about the sources of information. Avoid plagiarism and always give proper credit when citing sources. Do not copy and paste from sites like Wikipedia.

5. Lastly, remember to regularly update the security tools installed on your computer to protect yourself, your personal information, and your computer from viruses, spyware, and spam.

Additional Resources:

National Cyber Security Alliance: http://www.staysafeonline.org/
NCSA's mission is to educate and empower a digital society to use the Internet safely and securely at home, work, and school, protecting the technology individuals' use, the networks they connect to, and our shared digital assets. Their website provides educational materials and opportunities to engage in the digital movement.

Volunteer's bill of rights and responsibilities from Idealist.org:
http://idealist.org/volunteer/rightsresponsibilities.html
Idealist provides a helpful guide to how to volunteer responsibly and what to expect from a
volunteer opportunity.

*"In every community there is work to be done. In every nation, there
are wounds to heal. In every heart, there is the power to do it."*

Marianne Williamson
Author, spiritual activist, and founder of The Peace Alliance

*"Every individual matters. Every individual has a role to play. Every
individual makes a difference. And we have a choice: What sort of
difference do we want to make?"*

Jane Goodall
Anthropologist and UN Messenger of Peace

Chapter 7: Maintaining Motivation & Energy

"Find something concrete that keeps you coming back. Regardless of the other demands on my time, I know that talking to that little girl who wants to be a soccer player when she grows up (just like I did) over granola bars and juice boxes will be the best part of my week."

Trisha Macrae, University of Chicago

Rachel Cohen loves animals. Once in college, she wanted to continue volunteering for an animal shelter playing with puppies just as she did on Wednesday afternoons in high school. However, she ended up helping the animal shelter to put down stray dogs in Philadelphia—a far cry from spending time with adorable creatures.

Rachel spent a summer agonizing about the meaning of her work and questioning its value. She stuck it out, trusting that the organization's commitment to animal rights meant that their work was ultimately creating a positive impact.

She's continued to volunteer with them and recently came up with a new idea for the shelter. Now Rachel runs an innovative program that brings animals from the shelter to play with kids from a local homeless shelter. The kids come alive when playing with these furry creatures! Rachel managed to creatively refocus on what she loves about working with animals to ensure the right sort of satisfaction from her volunteer work.

Points to Remember

- Whenever possible, be a "solutions" person rather than a problems person, and try to turn obstacles into opportunities.
- Communicate regularly with your supervisor or another reliable adult at your volunteer site.
- Understand the "WHY" of your service and your organization.
- Take quick notes after each session.
- Celebrate milestones.

What are your strengths?

Whether in class, on a sports field, at work, or at your community service site, knowing personal strengths helps you bring value everywhere you go. Get started identifying yours through leadership or personality assessments, like the Myers-Briggs Type Inventory or Strengthsquest. Strengthsquest, based on Positive Psychology, uses the Clifton StrengthsFinder to help students establish their top five strengths. Your strengths report comes with recommendations on how to use your strengths in school and at work.

Try taking one of these inventories and then think about applying your strengths as a volunteer. As you look for volunteer sites, take your strengths into consideration. For example, if you are outgoing and love talking to people, you might enjoy volunteering in a classroom or for large events, while someone who prefers peace and quiet and one-on-one interaction might make a great mentor or office volunteer for a nonprofit organization.

PRACTICAL TIPS:

✓ Schedule regular check-ins with your supervisor; adopt the practice of discussing what's going well *and* what you'd like to improve or change. If you get used to talking about little problems then you'll be able to handle talking about bigger ones if the need arises.

✓ Take five minutes to make notes about what you did and how you feel *each time* you volunteer. Review your notes before your meeting with your supervisor.

✓ If a task seems repetitious, mindless, or boring, ask for help—even the most menial tasks, like sorting clothes or canned food, can be fun if you take the time to get to know someone while doing them.

It's the end of the second half of an intense soccer game. Your team was down at the half and you missed a pass. Someone rallied, you scored a goal, and your team won the game in the last minute! One way to think about your volunteer experience is like being on a sports team that just won. Though you come out on top, there were ups and downs. Despite those foibles, your team won and at the end of the game you experienced the great feeling that comes with winning.

As a volunteer, you will have ups and downs. Since you're working with kids, animals, elderly people, and special-needs populations, no one knows exactly what will happen each day. Even with internships or "indirect" volunteer experiences, you're still interfacing with supervisors and staff members. You won't be able to anticipate every interaction. Still, with a few simple tips you can create the most successful experience possible. Let's explore ways you can find motivation in your volunteer work, so even the lowest lows are just a part of the journey to a big win at the end.

Volunteering is an inspiring experience. You are doing your part to change the world! As a volunteer, your motivation at times will be *extrinsic*—coming from the work you're doing and the people you're helping. You also need to draw upon *intrinsic* motivation—motivation from within. Volunteering also helps you come to know what you like and don't like, and to identify strengths you bring to the table.

Part One: Tips for Motivated Volunteering

TIP ONE: USE YOUR STRENGTHS

In Chapter 2, we discussed identifying what interests and motivates you. Regardless of what volunteer work you decide to pursue, knowing and engaging in work related to your personal interests is important to maintain motivation. Do you get energized by talking to people? Does playing with animals make you smile? Do you love organizing things? Are you interested in sports, music, recycling, or math? Do you have a creative impulse to paint? Figure out what excites you and look for opportunities to apply these within a volunteer setting.

TIP TWO: DOCUMENT YOUR WORK & CELEBRATE MILESTONES

Throughout your time as a volunteer you'll make progress. Whether you're a one-day or year-round volunteer, you will make small and large contributions. Stay motivated by keeping track of both the work you're doing and your initial and ongoing reactions to your work. Commit to taking 5-10 minutes after each volunteer session to jot down a few quick notes about what you did, what you accomplished, and how you felt. Whenever you need motivation, read your notes and review on what you've accomplished.

Just as important as documenting the work is celebrating. Every two or three weeks, pause to reflect on what you've done. Celebrating even the small meaningful moments is part of recognizing the value of your participation. As a volunteer in a first grade classroom, if your goal is helping a student learn to read by the year's end, celebrate when she learns how to read just one word or a whole sentence. Sharing the work you're excited about with your supervisor, a friend, or fellow volunteer builds relationships with people who share your interest in volunteering.

TIP THREE: ENGAGE IN REGULAR CONTACT WITH YOUR SUPERVISOR

Your supervisor should be ensuring you have a great and meaningful experience. Depending on how long you spend at your site each week, a bi-weekly or monthly check-in with your supervisor makes sense. Having an established meeting time from the onset means that if a problem comes up, you don't have to go out of your way to track down your supervisor—the time is already arranged. By building a strong relationship with your supervisor, he or she will get to know you well enough to provide valuable feedback and suggestions.

TIP FOUR: GIVE YOURSELF PERMISSION TO HAVE GOOD AND BAD DAYS

If you are expecting every day as a volunteer to be the same, think again. Sometimes you may leave saying, "I learned so much more from the experience than I was able to give today." Other times you will feel like you hit a home run. Even at the best possible volunteer site, every day isn't going to be amazing. That's okay and perfectly normal. Aim for great days and know that "good" and "bad" days (or moments) happen. Sometimes even the most fun or meaningful activities can become "boring" when they done over and over. Sometimes you'll leave feeling inspired. Sometimes work will be really hard and you'll make an unexpected breakthrough. Sometimes you'll be exposed to inequity or injustice that will deeply affect you. Those moments are part of the process. As you go into your experience, give yourself permission to have ups and downs, and figure out how to process the down days—talking to your supervisor or a friend, or writing in your journal are two ways to do this. What other ways can you think of?

Part Two: Seeing the Bigger Picture

Remember, there's a reason you chose this volunteer site over other options. As exciting or important as the placement might have seemed at the beginning, sometimes excitement fades over time. Try these three ways to revive your volunteer spirit:

(1) Find a friend or co-worker to join you.
(2) Understand the work you're doing in the context of the bigger picture.
(3) Check in with your supervisor, as mentioned in Tip Three above; explain that you need a cure for your diminished enthusiasm and ask for advice.

Another option is to look for a way to achieve balance when some of the work seems mundane or routine. A conversation with one of the founders, directors or volunteer coordinator can add depth to your understanding of the people and organization with whom you're working. Ask the volunteer coordinator who might be available to tell the organization's story. If you work with a number of volunteers, you could arrange for a gathering that instills everyone with a better sense of the organization and the work at hand.

See if you can connect the dots to a bigger picture by learning more about your organization and how you are contributing to their work and mission: *What is the ultimate vision or mission of your organization? Who do they impact and how? Where do you play a role in the organization's work? What are you learning? Do you feel like you're helping?* Knowing what the work you're helping with will ultimately *do* will make it worthwhile.

Part Three: Making Changes at Your Volunteer Site

Three introspective questions can help maintain motivation at your site: *What are you learning? In what ways are you contributing? Who and what at the site inspires **you**?* If answers are forthcoming then you can be assured of progress and productivity. If not, perhaps a change is necessary. You can change either your approach to what you are doing or change your work. Some of the tips in the last section like adding context to your work or finding the bigger picture might help you adjust your approach.

If a lack of learning or sense of contributing is the issue, discuss your work with your supervisor. Be prepared to articulate *why* you'd like to switch tasks or responsibilities. Remember that as a volunteer, you're ultimately there to help the organization—if you're able to do something that you enjoy then you'll be better able to contribute. Frame your request positively by highlighting what you will be able to contribute and learn in a new role. Be specific about your experience. The reaction could surprise you—maybe your supervisor has other important projects or tasks needing to be done, and didn't realize your interests were a better match for those activities. The reassignment may turn out to be a win-win situation. This is another reason to develop a relationship through scheduled conversations with your volunteer coordinator or supervisor from the beginning.

In some instances, volunteers decide to leave their volunteer site before their commitment was scheduled to end. Sometimes this is for unexpected personal reasons or because of a situation at the site. If you believe that you cannot continue to volunteer, make sure you have conversations with your supervisors or trusted adult before leaving.

Yes, volunteering has ups and downs, and hopefully the ups far outweigh the downs, providing a positive experience for you and the people you're serving! By using a few helpful tips, you can take large steps to make sure you're getting the most out of your volunteer experience.

Additional Resources:

Myers-Briggs Test: http://www.myersbriggs.org/my-mbti-personality-type/mbti-basics/

The Myers-Briggs Type Indicator (MBTI) assessment is a psychometric questionnaire designed to measure psychological preferences in how people perceive the world and make decisions. The MBTI is widely used as a leadership and professional development tool.

StrengthsQuest: https://www.strengthsquest.com/

StrengthsQuest is an online tool that generates a customized report detailing your top five talent themes, along with action items for development and suggestions on how to use your talents to achieve academic, career, and personal success. The assessment has been used by over 5 million people internationally.

"The more you lose yourself in something bigger than yourself, the more energy you will have."

Dr. Norman Vincent Peale
Author of The Power of Positive Thinking

"The best way to find yourself is to lose yourself in the service of others."

Mohandas Gandhi
Leader of the Indian independence movement and proponent of nonviolent civil resistance

Chapter 8: Reviewing What You're Learning, Gaining Perspective

"Whether you travel across the globe to volunteer in the developing world, or you donate food to a food pantry in your home town, the most incredible thing about service is the invaluable knowledge you gain in the process of giving back."

Lily Shaffer, Global Citizen Year Fellow

In 2008, the Community Service Coordinators at Phillips Academy Andover received grant funding to launch LASSO, the Lawrence Andover Special Service Opportunity program. LASSO invited students to participate in service and learning. Each of three groups tackled a different issue by doing service with an area nonprofit and bringing an expert faculty member along as well. Andover philosophy teacher Andy Housiaux conducted a session on the purpose of education and its current state with students who spent the afternoon working with kids from the Lawrence Youth Development Organization. Students, faculty, and community partners gathered together to serve and learn how their action impacts broader social issues.

Points to Remember

- You have a reason for volunteering.
- Strive to understand your impact and the impact of the organization.
- Consider: What? So What? Now What?

Whether doing community service for a scholarship or requirement, or to participate in your community, volunteering introduces a lifetime of being involved in changing the world. In this chapter, we'll explore types of service and how they relate to what all volunteers are ultimately striving to do: make a difference. As you think about your impact as a volunteer, start thinking about how you can continue to make an impact. Something as "small" as recruiting a great volunteer for your organization adds another contributor giving perhaps 20-30 hours of time—this adds up!

Part One: Reviewing What You're Doing

When volunteering, it's easy to get lost in the day-to-day routine. As you begin to look back on your work, here are some helpful ways to take stock and connect to the bigger picture.

Get started with three easy questions: *What? So what?* and *Now what?*[xiv] These questions are commonly paired with community service to help participants think about how to channel their experiences into action or next steps. Answer them on your own or with other volunteers.

Included with the questions is an example of how a student volunteering at an elementary school might respond at the end of their experience.

What?

How would you describe the actual work you've been doing? Whether it's playing with kids or talking to an elderly person or filing hospital records, describe your day-to-day work.

This term, I helped in a classroom every Tuesday for an hour. I read books with kids who were struggling with reading and writing and helped with spelling words. Sometimes I quizzed them or played games to help them with retention. While reading, we often talked about the stories and the characters.

So what?

What did these actions mean? Who did they impact? How did they affect the community you worked with? How did they contribute to the larger impact your organization is making?

Though I only worked with a few kids each week, I realized that my work also impacted the teacher. She could spend more time with other students in class and the kids I worked with were better prepared for their reading and spelling lessons after working with me. I was surprised by how well the kids responded. At first, they seemed really shy and distant. After a few weeks they started to jump up and smile when I walked. My volunteer coordinator explained that many kids at this school have unstable home lives and deal with a lot of change, so having a regular, recurring role model is especially valuable. I never realized the importance of just showing up each week!

Now what?

Now that you've done your service, what are you going to do next? Are there other channels of involvement? What else would you like to know about your site or issue? How will you take this experience and put it to use helping others?

When I talked to the teacher about my students, I learned about their backgrounds and other factors contributing to their low performance. I'd like to learn more about how to prevent the "achievement gap" that the teacher started to explain. My professor suggested taking a class on social issues in our Sociology department. I'd also like to volunteer with younger kids, so I've looked into volunteering at a local Head Start pre-school where maybe my efforts could help kids before they start to fall behind. I'd like to learn more strategies for helping kids learn to read. Another volunteer told me about a program where kids who have trouble reading can read to puppies, rather than adults, to get over their fear of reading. I'd really like to start a program like that!

Learning More: Who else is contributing?

There are 1.8 million organizations or nonprofits in the United States (see notation in Chapter 2), making up what is known as the nonprofit sector, the independent sector, or the third sector. As people and organizations get creative about approaching social problems, the lines between the sectors are blurring. The development of social entrepreneurship and social businesses are two examples of hybrids between principles of the social sector and the private sector.

A fascinating way to find out more about the issue your organization is addressing is to ask: *Who else is helping or hindering the work that we're doing?* Look at what private sector (business, organization, or government) efforts are working for or against your organization's mission. Your supervisor or other employees at your site might be able to tell you more about the others on the scene.

Part Two: Why What You Are Learning Matters
Through service, you are connecting to social issues

There are many ways that community service and service-learning contribute to creating positive social change. Whether you are doing service-learning and are involved in direct or indirect service, research, or advocacy, or you are performing community service for a school or scholarship requirement, or just for fun... you are aware that your efforts are helping to change the world for the better.

As you probably observed during your volunteer work, social change does not happen in a vacuum—there are many players involved and many approaches to tackling social issues.

Think about the issue of hunger. Every year in the Boston area, thousands of people participate in the *Walk for Hunger*. Each walker gets sponsors who contribute money for the 20-mile walk (indirect service), ultimately contributing millions of dollars donated to Project Bread, an anti-hunger nonprofit that serves people in need in the greater Boston area. Funds raised supports shelters and kitchens around the city, where volunteers serve meals every night of the year (direct service). Also, Project Bread releases statistics and fact sheets about hunger (research), coordinates awareness-raising events for politicians, and makes information about hunger readily available to the public (advocacy).[xv]

Each example tackles the issue of hunger in the Boston area, and each makes a significant impact. However, each highlights a different approach to addressing social issues: indirect service (the *Walk for Hunger),* direct service (preparing meals), research (collecting data and releasing compiling fact-sheets), and advocacy (bringing the issue to the public attention). These efforts are interrelated: when they work together, they are most effective.

Just as social "problems" occur on personal, cultural/institutional levels, so do the solutions. For example, when thinking of the social "problem" of homelessness, one might "blame" the individual, thinking that the reason that they are living in poverty without a stable job or place to live is because they are "lazy." However, it is important to realize that there are strong cultural and institutional factors at play, including a difficult economy where there are few jobs available for low-skilled workers as well as a lack of affordable housing. Solutions are vast and varied, from personal to cultural/institutional: from serving meals, to providing temporary shelter, to helping individuals apply for jobs, to subsidizing long-term housing, to government policies that incentivize employment.

When students serve, their efforts may be focused on creating change among individuals or cultures/institutions, or some combination of the two. Oftentimes the looking at the cultural/institutional levels of social issues can be overwhelming, and the personal level can seem like a tiny drop in the bucket of creating change. When working at the level of individual change (for example, tutoring a child, mentoring a young person who is at-risk, or helping an individual who is disabled), it is important to remember that your efforts do count. Loren Eiseley, in his 1969 essay *The Star Thrower*, touched on this idea. His original work has been adapted and retold countless times over the years, and now exists in the public domain as a short anecdote called *The Starfish Story*. Even with a modern twist, the sentiment remains the same:

> Thousands of starfish washed ashore.
> A little girl began throwing them in the water so they wouldn't die.
> "Don't bother, dear," her mother said, "it won't make a difference."
> The girl stopped for a moment and looked at the starfish in her hand.
> "It will make a difference to this one."

When working for cultural change, focus on how your efforts, combined with others, together make a difference. And when working for institutional change, focus on how policies, laws, and practices transform social structures (like the Civil Rights Act of 1964 that outlawed race-based segregation in the United States).

Ways to learn more about the importance of what you're doing and who else is doing similar work include:

The Internet: Google, Twitter, Facebook

Publications: Magazines (such as *GOOD* and *Beyond Profit*), daily newspapers, and socially relevant films

People: Employees of exciting nonprofit organizations, and speakers at a local university,

The Arts: Art exhibits, plays, musical performances, films, and books

Part Three: Service-Learning

Service-Learning

According to Cathryn Berger Kaye, the widely recognized authority on service-learning, in her book *The Complete Guide to Service-Learning:*

> Service learning can be defined in part by what it does for students. When service learning is used in a structured way that connects classroom content, literature, and skills to community needs, students will:

- apply academic, social, and personal skills to improve the community.
- make decisions that have real, not hypothetical, results.
- grow as individuals, gain respect for peers, and increase civic participation.
- experience success no matter what their ability level.
- gain a deeper understanding of themselves, their community, and society.
- develop as leaders who take initiative, solve problems, work as a team, and demonstrate their abilities while and through helping others.

In a school context and in other learning situations, service-learning can be defined as a research-based teacher method where guided or classroom learning is applied through action that addresses an authentic community need in a process that allows for youth initiative and provided structured time for reflection on the experience and demonstration of acquired skills and knowledge (9).

Six Stages of Service-Learning[xvi]

A growing number of high school and college students are engaging in service-learning as part of their courses. According to Cathryn Berger Kaye, there are five stages of service-learning, with a sixth often added to include the idea of student involvement in evaluation.

1. Inventory and Investigation

Using interviewing and other means of social analysis, students:

- catalog the interests, skills, and talents of their peers and partners.
- identify a need.
- analyze the underlying problem.
- establish a baseline of the need.
- begin to accumulate partners.

2. Preparation and Planning

With guidance from their teacher, students:

- draw upon previously acquired skills and knowledge.
- acquire new information through varied, engaging means and methods.
- collaborate with community partners.
- develop a plan that encourages responsibility.
- recognize the integration of service and learning.
- become ready to provide meaningful service.
- articulate roles and responsibilities of all involved.
- define realistic parameters for implementation.

3. Action

Through direct service, indirect service, research, advocacy, or a combination of these approaches, students take action that:

- has value, purpose, and meaning.
- uses previously learned and newly acquired academic skills and knowledge.
- offers unique learning experiences.
- has real consequences.
- offers a safe environment to learn, to make mistakes, and to succeed.

4. Reflection

During systematic reflection, the teacher or students guide the process using various modalities, such as role play, discussion, and journal writing. Participating students:

- describe what happened.
- examine the difference made.
- discuss thoughts and feelings.
- place experience in a larger context.
- consider project improvements.
- generate ideas.
- identify questions.
- encourage comments from partners and recipients.
- receive feedback.

5. Demonstration

Students showcase what and how they have learned, along with demonstrating skills, insights, and outcomes of service provided to an outside group. Students may:

- report to peers, faculty, parents, and/or community members.
- write articles or letters to local newspapers regarding issues of public concern.
- create a publication or Website that helps others learn from students' experiences.
- make presentations and performances.
- create displays of public art with murals or photography.

6. Evaluation

Students reflect on the project process to determine the areas where the project was successful and identify areas for improvement.

Benefits of Service-Learning

As mentioned in the first definition of service-learning, above, there are many ways that being involved positively impacts students, as well as educators, schools, organizations, the recipients of the service, and communities. The benefits may vary depending on how the service-learning experience is designed and carried out. Kaye explains that "service learning is known to promote resilience, empowerment, prosocial behaviors, motivation for learning, and engagement. These are mediators of academic success and help create the conditions for students to do better academically" (Kaye, 252). Additionally, students may gain skills and qualities that are rated as most important to future employers, including: communication skills, a strong work ethic, initiative, interpersonal skills, problem-solving skills, and teamwork skills (NACE, 23[xvii]).

Through service-learning, students may:[xviii]

- increase motivation and desire to learn.
- develop responsibility, think critically, make decisions, and solve problems.
- improve academic knowledge and performance, including writing and communication skills.
- cultivate self-perception.
- develop ability to work well with others.
- experience reciprocity.
- replace stereotypes with respect for others.
- interact with adults who have different roles in society.
- be exposed to career options including those in public service.
- become more knowledgeable about their community and the resources available for themselves and their families.
- experience civic responsibility.
- begin to develop a lifelong commitment to public service and to learning.

Through service-learning programs, communities can:

- increase resources to address problems and concerns.
- lend expertise in a particular issue area.
- become more knowledgeable about school programs and needs.
- collaborate in planning service-learning projects.
- participate in student learning.
- publicly acknowledge the contributions of young people.

PRACTICAL TIPS:

✓ Each time you volunteer, take a few minutes to make notes about what you did, what you learned, and how the experience impacted you.

✓ Engage in conversation with others to explain what you've been doing and why it's important. If you are in to photography, ask your supervisor if it's okay for you to take photos while volunteering (as there may be strict rules requiring permission and releases) and if permitted, enjoy documenting your adventures in service.

✓ If you are interested in learning more, ask people at your volunteer site about other people and groups that are doing similar work and then get to know them (attend events, set up informational interviews, and other opportunities).

Additional Resources:

http://www.Good.is
GOOD is the integrated media platform for people who want to live well and do good. GOOD is a company and community for the people, businesses, and NGOs moving the world forward. GOOD currently produces a website, videos, live events, and a print magazine. In 2010, GOOD started GOOD Projects — a new kind of agency focused on helping businesses and organizations do well by doing good.

http://www.SocialEdge.org
Social Edge is the global online community where social entrepreneurs and other practitioners of the social benefit sector connect to network, learn, inspire, and share resources. Social Edge is associated with the Skoll Foundation.

"Each time a person stands up for an ideal, or acts to improve the lot of others, he sends forth a tiny ripple of hope, and crossing each other from a million different centers of energy and daring, those ripples build a current that can sweep down the mightiest walls of oppression and resistance."

Robert F. Kennedy
U.S. Senator, 64th U.S. Attorney General, and civil rights activist

"If you don't like the way the world is, you change it. You have an obligation to change it. You just do it one step at a time."

Marian Wright Edelman
President and founder of the Children's Defense Fund

Chapter 9: Moving On Without Leaving a Hole in Your Heart or Theirs

"The final day of the service-learning project was bittersweet: it was amazing to see the students' pride in the work we helped them create, and yet it was so difficult to say goodbye to kids we'd spent a term building relationships with. Yet, the difficulty in ending a service project is countered by the progress and growth the students and volunteers have experienced together."

Victoria Wilmarth, Robertson Scholar at Duke University

Tori Wilmarth went to South Lawrence East Elementary School every week to excite third-graders about writing as part of her high school's Bread Loaf Pen Pals program. The high school's semester schedule was different from the elementary school schedule, so each term Tori and her fellow volunteers needed to end their volunteering with the elementary school students before the students' semester was over. Tori took all the steps necessary to make sure the teachers and students knew about her departure well in advance. As a result, the students, volunteers, and teachers could all celebrate the time they had together, rather than being sad or disappointed about the volunteers' departure. Tori's efforts included:

- Telling the teachers in advance
- Telling the students, "You know, next week is my last week."
- Writing thank you notes to the teachers
- Helping the Bread Loaf program organize a special end-of-term field trip to her high school

Now, even though Tori is in college, she returns for events when she's back in town over holidays. She also continues to recommend the program to younger students and volunteers.

PRACTICAL TIPS:

✓ Write thank-you notes to the people you worked with.

✓ Ask for a letter documenting your service.

How to Write a Stellar Thank-You Note

The best thank-you notes are simple and direct, acknowledging something great someone else has done to make your experience worthwhile. Unless your handwriting is really illegible, they should always be handwritten on note cards or personalized stationery.

A stellar thank-you note will not only say "thank you," but will also comment on specific details about the person you're thanking and how they made a difference. Try to stay away from generic terminology and remember that your goal is to take two or three sentences to leave the recipient smiling and remembering how amazing your time was.

An example written by a classroom volunteer might look like this:

Dear Mrs. Meyer,

Thank you so much for being my supervisor as a classroom volunteer this term. The highlight of my week is Tuesday mornings when I come into your classroom to spend time with your amazing students. At the beginning of the term you went out of your way to help me become a better reading tutor— your extra attention and efforts made my whole experience more worthwhile. I look forward to coming back to King Street Elementary for special events next term, and I will miss seeing you all each week. Thanks again!

Sincerely,
Barrett

Points to Remember

- Communication is key during your volunteer experience and becomes even more important when leaving any volunteer position.
- Volunteering can lay foundations for ongoing relationships.
- Document work you've done, for yourself and the organization,
- Your relationship with your agency doesn't end when you finish volunteering; spread the word about your experience.

Maintaining Contacts

Relationships developed as a volunteer are among the greatest takeaways of the experience, and a big part of why millions of people donate their time each year. You may want to stay in touch with your supervisor, the organization's founder and staff of your organization, the people you serve, and your fellow volunteers are all people with whom you might have a personal or professional interest in keeping in touch with after you leave. With personal contacts like kids you tutored or people you worked with in a community, first ask the policies and expectations of the organization you work with (as there may be liability issues with maintaining contact, especially with children) and then think about how you will realistically keep in touch. Try to resist making promises you can't keep. Using email or arranging for a follow-up visit (and following through!) are great ways to keep in touch without creating the potential awkwardness of something like giving a seven-year-old your phone number—which, again, may be in violations with the policies and regulations of the organization or agency you are serving.

With sites like LinkedIn and Facebook, keeping in touch is really easy, but do make sure to do it! You never know when you'll need a recommendation letter or an interview with a fascinating individual.

You've spent a lot of time and energy finding a volunteer opportunity and actually volunteering. Whether it has been an amazing experience or one that has not lived up to your expectations, your volunteer service will eventually come to end.

The transition process occurs in three stages: 1) what happens before you leave, 2) your departure, and 3) what happens after you leave.

Keep in mind:

- Communication is key to a smooth transition.
- Preserving the work you've done will help ensure your efforts are beneficial to the organization even after you leave.

Before You Leave

- Plan out a timeline.
- Figure out who will be affected.
- Prepare with your supervisor.

- Document your work for yourself and for the organization: could someone come in and start where you left off?

At least a few weeks before the end of your volunteer experience, you start to plan for your departure, aiming to make your exit as smooth as possible.

(1) Think about who will be affected by your departure.

Are you working with kids who will miss you? Does the elderly woman who says "hello" to you each week know you are leaving? Which staff members do you work with directly? With any population where you have been depended on as a regular participant, make sure to give plenty of notice before you leave. Saying something like, "We have two weeks left. Is there anything that you'd like to do before I leave?" will help people realize your timeframe and better prepare them for your last visit. If you'd like to stay in touch with anyone you've developed relationships with, think about how you'd like to keep in touch and confirm that your actions are in line with the policies of the organization. If you decide to give out your phone number, make sure you're ready for phone calls at any time of day or night!

(2) Prepare for your departure with your supervisor.

Many organizations have a departure protocol for volunteers that could include a check-out meeting, filling in an evaluation, or a formal farewell event. Even if your organization doesn't have a policy on what to do when you leave, check with supervisors well in advance to find out what they think you should do or complete prior to leaving.

(3) Document your work.

You have done work that will need to survive beyond your time at the organization, so take time to create the proper documentation. If you have had any particular responsibilities or assignment, consider what documentation would be helpful as a courtesy to the organization or future volunteers. If you wrote a proposal, keeping a copy (with permission from the organization) could be valuable the next time you have to do a similar assignment. Maybe a description of the Earth Day event you helped organize with your third grade classroom would be a great add to a scholarship essay. Documentation in words, photos (where appropriate), or video help the organization learn what went well and what could be improved about your volunteer experience.

Be sure to present this documentation to your supervisor, so that he or she has specific examples of your work to reference when writing your recommendation letter!

Your Departure

Organizations vary on how they approach departures. Some have specific start and end dates for groups of volunteers and others rotate people in and out on a rolling basis. Regardless of your organization's approach, you can create your own sense of finality as your last day approaches. Here are some suggestions or saying farewell

- Bring in cookies or treats for everyone on your last day.
- Arrange to say a group "thank you" to your team.
- Write thank you notes to people who have supported you along the way.

After You Leave

Can you stay connected or involved with the organization beyond the last day? So many possibilities! Past volunteers often continue their involvement by becoming employees, advocates, board members, or simply renewing their relationship as volunteers, even if on a reduced time basis. There are numerous ways to stay involved—most important is to keep in touch.

- Join the organization's email list or subscribe to their newsletter.
- Volunteer to help at out special events that take minimal time while showing your remain committed to their cause.
- If you have developed any long-term relationships, keep in touch with updates of what you are doing both in school and your professional ambitions; this can be helpful when seeking recommendation letters, internships, job placements, and leadership opportunities.

Are you now a fan of this organization? Did your experience stand our as memorable and worthwhile? Then, spread the word! Let the world know about what you did and saw! Here are a few suggestions:

- If you enjoyed your experience, tell others about the opportunity to volunteer. An endorsement to your teacher or school volunteer program could help recruit more quality volunteers.

- Write about the organization and your experience for your school or local newspaper, a blog, or a magazine.
- Offer to speak at upcoming events on behalf of the organization. You could even reach out to community organizations like Rotary or Kiwanis or youth groups to make a presentation.

Additional Resources:

http://www.serve.gov/share.asp
United We Serve and the Corporation for National and Community Service invite all Americans to share their community service stories. The campaign highlights what Americans, young and old, are doing to strengthen their communities.

http://www.youtube.com/nonprofits
Nonprofits can establish their own channel on YouTube enabling them to use video, a powerful medium, to share their organization's impact and needs with the YouTube online community.

*"We make a living by what we get,
but we make a life by what we give."*

Winston Churchill
Former British Prime Minister

"I don't know what your destiny will be, but one thing I do know: the only ones among you who will be really happy are those who have sought and found how to serve."

Albert Schweitzer
Theologian, philosopher, Nobel Peace Prize winner

Chapter 10: Resources for More Information

"I came away inspired to go out into the world, pursue my passion, and make change. I can no longer be content with sitting on the sidelines."

Zahra Bhaiwala, Columbia University

If you are inspired to create your own social action project or nonprofit/community organization, see these resources:

DoSomething.org has **Social Action Trainings,** to help students create Social Action Projects. They provide information online and hold in-person Social Action Bootcamps. See: http://www.dosomething.org/training.

Check out **Impact, Inc.**, created by Ashoka's Youth Venture (a Facebook-based game designed to teach you how the nonprofit world works), a youth serving organization. See: http://impact-inc.org/.

Ashoka's Youth Venture guides youth in launching their own lasting social ventures as leaders of social change. "Youth Venturers" start businesses, civil society organizations, and informal programs to address social issues such as poverty, health, the elderly, the environment, education, diversity, and the arts. See: http://labs.youthventure.org/.

Points to Remember

- There are many resources for volunteers, from people to websites to books.
- Volunteering with others can make your experience more fun and rewarding.

This book is intended to provide basic information, advice, and tips for student volunteers. Often the first experience volunteering is the most challenging, but once you get started with volunteering, you may quickly discover you hunger for more—more opportunities to create positive social change, and more information about the social, environmental, and economic issues you are addressing first-hand while volunteering. To help you stay involved, use these resources, from people to websites to books. While you can find endless information by entering "volunteering," "community service," or "service-learning" on a search engine, here you will find a select list of information for your future as a volunteer and change-maker.

People

Begin with people as the best source for information. The stories of their volunteer experiences are more compelling than words on a page. Speak to as many people as you can about your interest in becoming a volunteer—share your ideas, your interests, your questions, and your fears. Be aware that you may receive misinformation or someone else's experience may not be anything like your own. It's still best to start with people you know and whose advice you trust, including:

Friends

Parents & family members

Teachers

Coaches

Advisors

Guidance counselors

Neighbors

Friends' parents

Parents' friends

Other important people in your life (perhaps your former babysitter, or a religious figure like a minister, rabbi, or mullah)

Websites

These websites help volunteers get involved in their communities:

1-800-Volunteer: http://www.1-800-volunteer.org/

This national database of volunteer opportunities, powered by a volunteer management system for nonprofits, allows you to search for a place to volunteer or help in your local community. Once you complete the online interest form, organizations will contact you.

All for Good: http://www.allforgood.org/

All for Good is an online database of volunteer opportunities and nonprofit organizations associated with the Points of Light organization. All for Good also offers mobile applications.

America's Natural and Cultural Resources Volunteer Portal: http://www.volunteer.gov/

Volunteer.gov is a one-stop recruitment internet-based website where individuals can search for volunteer opportunities by the following criteria: volunteer activity, location of opportunity, effective date of the opportunity, the sponsoring partner and by keyword search.

The Website offers thousands of volunteer opportunities focused mostly on issues related to natural resources and Veteran's health

Ashoka's Youth Venture: http://www.genv.net/

Ashoka's Youth Venture helps teams of people start new youth-led organizations. GenV.net is a website with access to resources for coming up with ideas to start social ventures and provides resources to support them.

Campus Compact: http://www.campuscompact.org/

Campus Compact is a resource designed to help college students become active citizens and respond to challenging societal issues. For more than twenty years, Campus Compact has engaged more than 20 million students in service and service-learning. Campus Compact has a presence on many college campuses in the United States.

DoSomething.org: http://www.dosomething.org/actnow/volunteer

Do Something provides organizations and volunteers with a user-friendly online platform. Students can browse opportunities and see featured projects started by young people. Do Something also provides grant funding and support for youth projects.

Idealist Volunteer Opportunities: http://idealist.org/if/as/vol

Idealist.org is a comprehensive online database of volunteer opportunities domestically and abroad, internships, and employment opportunities with nonprofits and community organizations.

National Youth Leadership Council: http://www.nylc.org/

NYLC has as its mission empowering youth to transform themselves from recipients of information and resources into valuable, contributing members of a democracy through service-learning. Every year, about 2000 people attend the National Service-Learning Conference, and NYLC has been a leader in establishing the current national standards for K-12 service-learning.

NobleHour.com: http://www.NobleHour.com/

Noble Hour is an online community engagement platform that allows students to find opportunities, log their hours, and track and measure their impact.

Nonprofit Leadership Alliance: http://www.humanics.org/

The Nonprofit Leadership Alliance provides training, resources, support, and certification in Nonprofit Leadership and Management. Many colleges and universities offer academic certification through NLA.

Play Interrobang: http://playinterrobang.com/

InterroBang?! is a game where you get to have fun with problems. Students complete real-world missions with deeds that can win prizes, improve problem solving skills, and connect them with others to do things that just might change the world.

Random Kid: http://www.randomkid.org/

This organization was started in response to the Hurricane Katrina disaster by then 10 year old Talia Leman. In the past five years, her website has mobilized 12 million kids to raise $11 million to to launch their own ventures to solve social problems.

U Give: http://www.ugive.org/

UGive is an online platform designed to facilitate volunteerism among students, schools, and nonprofits. UGive offers service transcripts to schools and students and an online tracking/reporting system.

United We Serve: http://www.serve.gov/

Serve.gov, managed by the Corporation for National and Community Service, is an online resource for finding and creating volunteer opportunities. United We Serve focuses specifically on growing social needs resulting from the economic downturn.

Volunteer Match: http://www.volunteermatch.org/

Volunteer Match is a national database of nonprofit and community organizations and volunteer opportunities across sectors and type. Log on to find out where you can volunteer in your city.

Youth Service America: http://www.ysa.org/

YSA is committed to improving communities by increasing the number and diversity of 5–25 year olds involved in their communities. YSA runs public mobilization campaigns, like Global Youth Service Day, provides funding and awards for service endeavors, and trains young people and educators around the country.

YouthNoise: http://www.youthnoise.com/

YouthNoise is an online forum with more than 170,000 registered users from all 50 states and 176 countries around the world. YouthNoise primarily works with low-income and under-represented youth ages 13 – 25. YouthNoise partners with Link TV and the Just 1 Click campaign to support youth service efforts virtually.

Books

Be the Change! Change the World. Change Yourself by Michelle Nunn, ed., Hundreds of Heads Books, 2006.

Be the Change celebrates the personal transformations of men and women who, by working to change the world, changed themselves. Featuring interviews with over 1,000 volunteers, from everyday people to business and community leaders to celebrities, the book combines hands-on advice on ways to get involved with real-life stories.

Giving from Your Heart, A Guide to Volunteering by Dr. Bob Rosenberg and Guy Lampard, iUniverse Inc, 2005.

How to get started as a volunteer? From determining your desired level of involvement to establishing realistic expectations, Rosenberg and Lampard offer practical information that will help you connect with the volunteer opportunity that's right for you.

How to Volunteer Like a Pro: An Amateur's Guide for Working with Teenagers by Jim Hancock, Zondervan/Youth Specialties, 2008.

After more than twenty years as a paid youth worker, Jim Hancock became a volunteer in a student ministry. Inside this book you'll find practical help, like: tips about what to do on the first day, ideas on how to build and develop relationships with students, ways to combat youth "culture shock," how to prepare students for life after youth group, how to say goodbye when it is time to leave, and other insights for working with youth.

The Idealist.org Handbook to Building a Better World: How to Turn Your Good Intentions into Actions that Make a Difference by Stephanie Land, ed., Perigree Trade, 2009.

Part career guide, part activist's handbook, this guide provides tools and inspiration for anyone who wants to make a difference but doesn't know where to start. Inspired by Idealist.org's 600,000-member online community and their ongoing search for work that gives back to the world, this practical reference walks readers through the different ways they can get involved and the range of possibilities for applying one's interests and skills to meet their community's needs.

Make a Difference: America's Guide to Volunteering and Community Service by Arthur I. Blaustein, Jossey-Bass, 2003.

This revised and expanded guide includes more than 185 national, nonprofit organizations that use volunteers of all ages to make a difference where it counts, plus 30 organizations that give up-to-date information on critical issues and policies.

Raise Your Voice: A Student Guide to Making Positive Social Change by Richard E. Cone, Abby Kiesa, and Nicholas V. Longo, eds., Campus Compact Publication, 2006.

This guide speaks directly to student leaders seeking to improve the effectiveness of their engaged work while enhancing academic and civic learning. Based on three years of activity in Campus Compact's hugely successful Raise Your Voice civic action campaign, which mobilized hundreds of thousands of students across the country, this book has targeted strategies, tools, and activities for organizing change on campus.

The Teen Guide to Global Action: How to Connect with Others (Near & Far) to Create Social Change by Barbara A. Lewis, Free Spirit Publishing, 2007.

This is a practical, hands-on guide for youth who want to make a difference, featuring inspiring stories of youth from over 30 countries who are taking action on local and global issues. Includes information, tips, tools, and activities to help young people create social change.

Volunteering: The Ultimate Teen Guide (It Happened to Me) by Kathlyn Gay, Scarecrow Press, 2007.

This resource guides teens to using their time and energy to positively impact society and gain personal satisfaction. Get a complete picture of what volunteering involves, including personal commitment and the physical and emotional stamina, as well as the positive, and sometimes negative, consequences. Inspiring and rewarding stories from teen volunteers who testify to the immense personal satisfaction from volunteer efforts.

You

You! You are your best resource. You are bright, capable, and energetic. You have a unique combination of gifts and talents. Your presence has the ability to bring light to the eyes of an elderly person or a smile to the face of a child. Volunteering can be transformative for everyone involved. Do not ignore or fear *your* ability to make a difference in the world. Adults often say that students are the leaders of tomorrow, but we believe that you can be leaders *today*, and getting involved in your community is a great first step.

"Go out into the world and do well, but more importantly, go out into the world and do good."

Minor Myers, Jr.
17th President of Illinois Wesleyan University

Appendix

Benefits of Community-Based Service-Learning[xix]

Thousands of community-based organizations engage millions of young people in service and service-learning. Though research in K-12 and higher education settings shows a wide range of benefits of effective service-learning (RMC Research, 2006), much less is known about the actual value or benefits of service and service-learning in community-based settings. This fact sheet highlights some of the emerging knowledge in this field based on theory, process evaluations, and field wisdom—knowing that more rigorous research is needed.

What Are Community-Based Organizations?

There are many kinds of community-based organizations, and there are many ways to define their scope. For purposes of this overview, community-based organizations include:

- Social service and other nonprofit providers or associations that may engage young people (and adults) as volunteers;
- Community-based youth development organizations and after-school programs that include service or service-learning as part of their programming; and
- Faith-based organizations that provide services and offer service experiences as part of their programming. (Because of the unique goals and context of faith-based organizations, the research from that sector is not included in this overview.)

Service and service-learning take many different forms in community settings. One study identified, for example, 11 different models in school-based programs and 15 different forms in community-based programs. These include a series of programs on a specific issue, short-term projects, summer programs, crisis response activities, and youth advisory and planning groups (Shumer, 1993). Hence, one size clearly does not fit all.

Benefits for Youth Participants

Youth who participate in high-quality community-based service-learning are likely to benefit in a number of ways (Chung, 1997; Coe-Regan et al, in press; Lewis-Charp et al., 2003; Tannenbaum, S. C., 2007; and YMCA of the USA, 2004):

- Young people gain access to the range of supports and opportunities (or developmental assets) they need to grow up healthy, caring, and responsible. One study of youth civic activism found that these settings had particular strength in cultivating youth and community involvement (Lewis-Charp et al., 2003).
- Increased sense of self-efficacy as young people learn that they can impact real social challenges, problems, and needs.
- Higher academic achievement and interest in furthering their education.
- Enhanced problem-solving skills, ability to work in teams, and planning abilities.
- Enhanced civic engagement attitudes, skills and behaviors. Many leaders in public service today speak about how they were nurtured, inspired, and shaped in early experiences in community service or volunteering.

Benefits for Youth Development Organizations

Youth development organizations and after-school programs that use service-learning can benefit from this strategy in a number of ways:

- Young people are more likely to stay engaged when they feel their participation is meaningful and they can make useful contributions through service and social action.
- Service-learning gives an intentional strategy for addressing goals for learning and personal development through civic engagement and community service.
- Service-learning can cultivate connections between the organization, schools, and other community groups.
- Service-learning can increase program staff and volunteers' level of engagement, leadership capacity, and satisfaction with their work.

It is also noteworthy that effective service-learning practices are closely aligned with effective youth development practices A major report from the National Research Council and Institute of Medicine (2002) identified eight factors in community programs that facilitate positive youth development:

- Physical and psychological safety;
- Appropriate structure;
- Supportive relationships;
- Opportunities to belong;
- Positive social norms;

- Support for efficacy and mentoring;
- Opportunities for skill building; and
- Integration of family, school, and community efforts.

Done well, service-learning programs addresses all these factors and becomes a particularly useful strategy for increasing self-efficacy and integrating family, school, and community efforts. (Also see Benson et al., 2006; Scales & Roehlkepartain, 2004).

Benefits to Organizations that Utilize Young People as Volunteers

Community-based organizations that engage young people in service and service-learning point to the following kinds of benefits (Chung, 1997, Roehlkepartain, 1995; Naughton, 2000; Melchoir, 1998; reinforced by the general research on the benefits of all types of volunteers identified in: Urban Institute, 2004):

- The opportunity to expand their mission and reach without substantially increasing costs by engaging a cadre of competent, motivated young people who share their time and talents in support of the organization's mission.
- New energy, ideas, and enthusiasm as well as specialized skills that young people can bring to the organization (such as community skills). Inca Mohamed writes, "Every young person, like every adult, has unique abilities and experience that can expand the capacities and outcomes of [social change] efforts" (Mohamed, 2001, p. 15).
- Increased public support and visibility in the community as young people become ambassadors for the agency in their schools, homes, and other networks.
- New partnerships and resources that emerge when agencies for service-learning partnerships with schools, youth development organizations, faith-based organizations or others that provide service-learning as part of their programming.
- By working with youth and getting them committed to its mission, an organization cultivates a new generation of volunteers for either their own organization or their broader cause.

Benefits for Service Recipients, Communities, and Society

Beyond the young people the organizations directly involve, community-based service-learning benefits the people served, their communities, and, ultimately, society:

- It meets real needs and priorities for individuals and communities, as young people bring new energy, capacity, and creative ideas.
- Community residents have opportunities to build positive relationships with young people.
- Communities see youth in a different way—as resources, not problems.
- A new generation of caring and experienced citizens, activists, and volunteers is cultivated (Mohamed & Wheeler, 2001).

Benefits Don't Come Automatically

The benefits outlined above are not automatic or universal. The specific benefits or impact will vary, depending on the focus, scope, and quality of a particular service or service-learning experience. And, based on other research, it is likely that the benefits are stronger (particularly for young people) for service-learning than for volunteering or community service. Thus, integrating core elements of effective service-learning is key to reaping these and other benefits. Among these core elements of effective practice are the following themes (RMC Research, 2007. Also see Naughton, 2000; and Mantooth & Hamilton, 2004):

- Young people have active and meaningful leadership roles;
- The program is guided by clear and intentional learning and development goals;
- Active, intentional, and structured reflection is integral to the program;
- Young people are involved across time (at least 20 hours across several months); and
- The service projects meet real community needs and priorities.

Conclusion

Community-based service-learning does not receive the kind of public attention that service-learning receives in education. Yet it offers significant benefits to society, to young people, and to participating institutions. Lawrence Neil Bailis and colleagues (2005) write:

> Schools are not the only institutions that educate our young people, and community-based organizations can be far more than the 'stage' that schools use to deliver the service-learning programs that they develop. Kindergarten-through-twelfth-grade schooling is only one format for 'education' where young people gain the knowledge, skills, attitudes, and aspirations they will need to become successful adults [p. 3].

References

Bailis, L. N., Shields, T., Henning, A., & Neal, M. (2005). *Profiles of community-based service-learning in the United States.* St. Paul, MN: National Youth Leadership Council. Retrieved from http://www.nylc.org/rc_downloaddetail.cfm?emoid=14:149

Benson, P. L., Scales, P. C., Hamilton, S. F., & Sesma, A., Jr. (2006). Positive youth development: Theory, research, and applications. In W. Damon & R. M. Lerner (Eds.), *Handbook of child psychology: Theoretical models of human development (6th ed.)* (Vol. 1, pp. 894-941).

Chung, A. N. (1997). Service as a strategy in out-of-school time: A how-to manual. Washington, DC: Corporation for National Service. Retrieved from http://nationalserviceresources.org/learns/service-ost

Coe-Regan, J. R., & O'Donnell, J. (2006). Best practices for integrating technology and service learning in a youth development program. *Journal of Evidence-Based Social Work, 3*, 201-220.

Eccles, J., & Gootman, J. A. (2002). Community programs to promote youth development. Washington, DC: National Academy Press.

Lewis-Charp, H., HanhCao Yu, H., Soukamneuth, S., & Lacoe, J. (2003). Extending the reach of youth development through civic activism: Research results from the youth leadership for development initiative. Takoma Park, MD: Innovation Center for Community and Youth Development.

Mantooth, L. J., & Hamilton, M. P. (2004). *4-H service learning standard and best practice guide.* Knoxville, TN: University of Tennessee Agricultural Extension Service. Retrieved from http://www.utextension.utk.edu/4h/SOS/resources/index.htm

Melchior, A. (1998). National evaluation of Learn and Serve America school and community-based programs: Final report. Washington, DC: Corporation for National and Community Service.

Mohamed, I. A. (2001). Notes from a program officer: The case for youth engagement. In I. Mohamed & W. Wheeler (Eds.), Broadening the bounds of youth development: Youth as engaged citizens. Takoma Park, MD: Innovation Center for Community and Youth Development.

Mohamed, I. A., & Wheeler, W. (Eds.). (2001). Broadening the bounds of youth development: Youth as engaged citizens. Takoma Park, MD: Innovation Center for Community and Youth Development.

Naughton, S. (2000). Youth and communities helping each other: Community-based organizations using service-learning as a strategy during out-of-school time. Washington, DC: Corporation for National Service.

RMC Research Corporation. (2006). *Impacts of service-learning on participating k-12 students.* Scotts Valley, CA: National Service-Learning Clearinghouse. Retrieved from http://www.servicelearning.org/instant_info/fact_sheets/k-12_facts/impacts/index.php

RMC Research Corporation. (2007). *Improving outcomes for k-12 service-learning participants.* Scotts Valley, CA: National Service-Learning Clearinghouse. Retrieved from http://www.servicelearning.org/instant_info/fact_sheets/k-12_facts/improving_outcomes/index.php

Roehlkepartain, E. C. (1995). Everyone wins when youth serve. Washington, DC: Points of Light Foundation.

Scales, P. C., & Roehlkepartain, E. C. (2004). Service to other: A "gateway" asset for school success and healthy development. In J. Kielsmeier, M. Neal, & M. McKinnon (Eds.), Growing to greatness 2004: The state of service-learning project (pp. 26-32). St. Paul, MN: National Youth Leadership Council.

Shumer, R. (1993). *Describing service-learning: A Delphi study.* St. Paul, MN: University of Minnesota, Department of Vocational and Technical Education.

Tannenbaum, S. C. (2007). Tandem pedagogy: Embedding service-learning into an after-school program. Journal of Experiential Education, *29*(2), 111-125.

Urban Institute. (2004). Volunteer management capacity in America's charities and congregations: A briefing report. Washington, DC: Author.

YMCA of the USA. (2004). The YMCA service-learning guide: A tool for enriching the member, the participant, the YMCA, and the community (2nd ed.). Chicago, IL: Author.

---

[i] http://www.nationalservice.gov/pdf/08_1112_lsa_prevalence.pdf page 10

[ii] "College student volunteering increased by approximately 20 percent between 2002 and 2005, as students have become involved in helping their communities," http://www.nationalservice.gov/about/role_impact/performance_research.asp#COLLEGE

[iii] "...set a goal that all middle school and high school students engage in 50 hours of community service a year," http://change.gov/americaserves/

[iv] "Require 100 Hours of Service in College: Establish a new American Opportunity Tax Credit worth $4,000 a year in exchange for 100 hours of public service a year," http://change.gov/agenda/service_agenda/

[v] The Idealist.org Handbook to Building a Better World: How to Turn Your Good Intentions into Actions that Make a Difference
Make a Difference: America's Guide to Volunteering and Community Service
Volunteering: The Ultimate Teen Guide (It Happened to Me)
Giving from Your Heart, A Guide to Volunteering
How to Volunteer Like a Pro: An Amateurs Guide for Working with Teenagers
Raise Your Voice: A Student Guide to Making Positive Social Change.
The Teen Guide to Global Action: How to Connect with others to Create Social Change
Be the Change. Change the World. Change Yourself

[vi] http://www.nationalserviceresources.org/practices/17451, handsonnetwork.org, campuscompact.org, http://www.volunteermatch.org/, idealist.org, http://www1.networkforgood.org/for-donors/volunteer

[vii] National Center for Charitable Statistics, http://nccsdataweb.urban.org/PubApps/profile1.php

[viii] http://www.nationalserviceresources.org/practices/17494
Jeff Woods, JUMP Coordinator, Sonoma State University in October 2002, offers guidelines that were developed by the City of Service Consortium Higher Education Service-Learning project and were originally distributed on the HE-SL (service-learning) email discussion list hosted by the National Service-Learning Clearinghouse.

[ix] Reprinted and adapted with permission from Adam Finck.
http://www.divinecaroline.com/article/22347/39163-wet-blanket-vs--martyr--kick-butt

[x] Lewis, Barbara A. *The Teen Guide to Global Action: How to Connect with Others to Create Social Change*. p. 14 Free Spirit Publishing, 2008.

[xi] http://www.independentsector.org/volunteer_time

[xii] Adapted from:
http://www.1-800-volunteer.org/1800Vol/volunteer-connections/VCContentAction.do?aNewsId=462410&vcId=86940
http://www.ucsd.edu/current-students/student-life/involvement/leadership/community-service/rights-and-responsibilities.html
impairment and safety from: http://www.utexas.edu/diversity/ddce/vslc/comsum.php

[xiii] Adapted from: www.linksysbycisco.com/static/content/20090626/teen_cybersafety.pdf
http://www.staysafeonline.org/content/middle-high-school

[xiv] Janet Eyler and Dwight E. Giles, Jr. *Where's the Learning in Service-Learning?* San Francisco: Jossey-Bass, 1999.

[xv] Project Bread. "About Hunger," http://www.projectbread.org/site/PageServer?pagename=abouthunger_main. Copyright 2005-2010. Accessed 15 May 2010.

[xvi] **Stages 1–5:** Berger Kaye, Cathryn. *The Complete Guide to Service Learning: Proven, Practical Ways to Engage Students in Civic Responsibility, Academic Curriculum, & Social Action*. Minneapolis: Free Spirit Publishing, 2010. Print.
Stage 6: generationOn http://www.generationon.org/

[xvii] National Association of Colleges and Employers. Job Outlook 2010. 23. Fig. 34.

[xviii] Berger Kaye, Cathryn. *The Complete Guide to Service Learning: Proven, Practical Ways to Engage Students in Civic Responsibility, Academic Curriculum, & Social Action*. Minneapolis: Free Spirit Publishing, 2010. Print.

[xix] Roehlkepartain, E.C. (2007). *Benefits of Community-Based Service-Learning*. Scotts Valley, CA: National Service-Learning Clearinghouse. http://www.servicelearning.org/library/resource/8543

Manufactured by Amazon.ca
Acheson, AB

15808862R00046